WHAT'S RACISM ABOUT?

Let's look at schools

Alan Sharp

Grosvenor House
Publishing Limited

This book is published by
Grosvenor House Publishing Ltd
Link House
140 The Broadway, Tolworth, Surrey, KT6 7HT.
www.grosvenorhousepublishing.co.uk

A CIP record for this book
is available from the British Library

ISBN 978-1-83975-806-5

DEDICATION

To Michael Williams
author, *Black scientists & Inventors* series
through whose initiative
many people of colour have said they wanted me
to write a version of my first book
Changing Generations
'but for schools'.
May the communities achieve their liberation!

'I grew up in Thornton Heath, south-east London. Although raised by a good family in a close community, I was exposed to violence and violent crime throughout my childhood and young adult life. I've seen people beaten and stabbed and shot. In 2011, I was involved in an incident where my mum was shot in front of me and my stepfather was shot and killed. I myself spent several years committing crimes, running from the police and, at one point, I went to jail. Although I now appreciate this is far from normal, we didn't know that almost daily violence wasn't the norm for most young British kids. I believe that we – me and my community – suffer from the trauma of what we experienced, to this day' (Konan, rapper, 2019).[1]

'It is only when you meet someone of a different culture from yourself that you begin to realise what your own beliefs really are' (George Orwell, 1937). Born Eric Arthur Blair, his Scottish ancestors were slave-owners in Jamaica from 1699 and married into the English ruling class. His great-great-grandfather, Charles Blair, in 1834 received £4,442 (£3 million in today's money), at the freeing of 218 enslaved Africans that he owned in St-Thomas-in-the-East. The loan raised by the British government to make this payment was only paid off by British taxpayers in 2015.[2]

About the Author

Alan Sharp worked as a Community Development Worker in Tooting, South London from 2000 until retirement in 2018. He holds a BA Hons in Modern History and Politics with Economics from Southampton University, an MBA from Manchester Business School and an RSA Certificate in Teaching English as a Foreign Language (TEFL) from International House, London. He has taught English to refugees in a language school and to international business people. He has also taught French to British children. He tweets on Twitter under the username @chggenerations.

He says that learning to see the world through the eyes of people of colour has led him to critique his own way of thinking. It's helped him to gain a white, antiracist identity. He is learning to work with white people in solidarity with people of colour so that people of colour can find liberation from oppression in this generation. His first book, Changing Generations, was published by BIS Publishing Services.

CONTENTS

INTRODUCTION

'I've been bullied ever since I started school. The bullies call me nasty names; it makes me feel so ashamed. My friends won't hang out with me anymore because people started asking why they were friends with someone who had dirty skin. I was born in the UK but bullies tell me to go back to my own country. I don't understand because I'm from the UK. I've tried to make my face whiter before using makeup so that I can fit in. I just want to enjoy going to school.' (10-year-old girl to NSPCC Childline, 2019).

'I'm being bullied at school because I'm Chinese. The other kids say that my skin is yellow, call me names, and it gets me really down. I hate the way I look so much; I think if I looked different everyone would stop being mean to me and I'd fit in. I've tried to change the way that I look by using eyeliner so that I fit in more. I don't want to tell my parents because I think it would upset them.' (11-year-old girl to NSPCC Childline, 2019).

'People call me a terrorist and keep telling me to go back to where I came from. I dress in traditional Muslim clothes and I think it singles me out. I usually just put my head down and get on with it but it's getting to the point now where I genuinely feel like I might get attacked.' (16-year-old girl from a Muslim background to NSPCC Childline, 2019).[3]

'Racism's ended now, hasn't it?'[4]

In a 2020 poll, people said racism in Britain had either got worse or stayed the same over their lifetime, rather than that racism was becoming less common. Nearly two-thirds of people thought there was a 'fair amount' or a 'great deal' of racism in Britain today.[5]

So what? As a man, if you're anything like me, you can't wait to get ahead of others and get rich. So, you elbow your way past other men to get to the front of the queue. 'I'm strong/he's weak.' 'I'm quick/he's slow.' 'I'm clever/he's sad.' It's called the master/slave relationship.[6] Then you elbow women out of the way. 'I'm rational/ she's emotional.' 'I'm tough/she's weak.'[7]

People of colour are people of African, Asian, Latin American and Pacific Islander backgrounds.[8] Your view may be that, 'I'm white. We're better than them. We've won two world wars and one World Cup.'[9] You feel you're invincible.

Until one day something goes wrong. Maybe you're made redundant and can't get back into work. Maybe your body packs up, or you experience abuse and get traumatised. You're feeling oppressed and you try to learn how other oppressed people are handling life. At last, you're open to learning from others.

As a baby, a person learns early, when learning what their self is, that their mother, who from time to time denies their baby's demands, is for them the object or 'the Other', and is different from the baby's self.[10]

So, when that person is older, they see those who are their family and community as their kindred. Advantaged individuals and groups determine that people see the foreigner, together with lower-class people and women, as 'the Other'. But it may be the foreigner who is suffering, for example by not living among their kindred. The challenge is to recognise that the person who is suffering is a human being, with an ancestor in common with you in Africa, and to be a friend to them.[11]

Learning to critique the way you think

- **for people of colour, your doing this is a life-or-death matter**

'On something as confusing as racism, is there any way I can check whether my way of thinking about racism is right?' Well, students learn to critique their way of thinking by learning from other people. People call this critical reflection.[12]

Now, if you want to understand sexism, you need to learn from women, the people who experience sexism. Similarly, if you want to understand racism, you need to learn from people of colour, the people who experience racism.

You do this by reading what people of colour write, rather than by hearing what they say. Because for many people, like women or people of colour, if they tell white men what they really think of them the relationship usually ends badly for themselves.[13] But people of colour have already written what they think of white people.

'How do you know how to critique me if you don't know what I'm like?' I don't know your personal identity. But part of identity relates to British identity. Colley suggests there are three ingredients of British identity, first Protestant culture, then the regular thrill of war, and finally the triumphs of the British Empire.[14] Currently, church attendance is low and falling. War in the last 430 years has mainly been to build and maintain the Empire. So, much of people's thinking about life is based on the version of the British Empire they have been taught over the years.

So, I'll try here to use a contemporary method through which people can critically reflect – postcolonial studies. Postcolonial studies is mainly people of colour looking at the consequences of white people's empire history for people of colour, whose ancestors white people colonised.[15]

'How come you think people of colour understand white people better than white people understand themselves?' Since very early in the lives of people of colour, white people have made them aware of their contempt for people of colour, and that white people will only allow white people to get the best things in life, while they leave what they don't want for people of colour.[16] So, people of colour now have a double consciousness: they know both what white people think about life and about people of colour, and what people of colour think about themselves.

In fact, people of colour were writing about whiteness (racism's effect on white people who act in a racist way) 200 years before Toni Morrison in 1990 showed how white American writers reacted in their books to African Americans living in America.[17] This finally prompted some white people to start finding out about their own whiteness.

- **every action has consequences**

In 2009, a 16-year-old youth who had been drinking killed 24-year-old Adam Rogers with a single punch.[18] Adam's parents started a charity called *Every action has consequences*, to show young people that drinking alcohol might have unexpected consequences.

It took me until I was in my 40s and made redundant a second time to realise that everything I had ever done had consequences. Until then, I had no concern about how people like me benefitted daily from complicity in a system that keeps me relatively rich by keeping most people in the world poor.

- **changing from anti-intellectualism to learning from what others write**

It's common for people to speak about issues, such as whether women should be allowed to have abortions, without stopping to read what other people have written about these issues. To speak about an issue by relying on what you see as 'common sense', rather than by reading first what people have written about it, is a practice known as anti-intellectualism.[19]

Anti-intellectualism is distrust of people seen as intellectuals who, because they have thought hard about issues, may come up with answers that might challenge the way people think and act. So, Michael Gove, when challenged about expert advice that said that Brexit could damage Britain's economy, said that he thought the 'people of this country have had enough of experts'.[20] Rich people may not like ordinary people knowing of those ideas because those ideas might change the system that currently works to rich people's advantage.

I have tried here not to write anything without first checking it with people who have studied these issues more than me. Their views are often different from those traditionally associated with the views of older, middle class, white men.

If you're concerned about changing inequality locally or abroad you could start by reading what's happening and how to change things for the better. 'This country could learn so much from the diverse people who now live here.'[21]

- **different life experiences lead to different standpoints**

If you're in a mountainous rural area, what you can see depends on where you're standing. You might only be able to see 50 metres along a winding, heavily-wooded stream and might not be able to tell others about what to do 5km away. To understand more about the bigger picture, you need to learn from people looking from different standpoints.[22]

People arrive at different standpoints through their different lived experiences. Lived experience is the experience of people on whom one or many social issues have had a personal impact. People gain knowledge and insights through their lived experience so they're able to drive for social change in their lives.[23]

For example, in the 1970s, many men saw women staying at home doing housework and raising children as women doing their natural work and labouring in love. Many women, however, saw their work for no income as exploited labour. They pointed to men presiding over a legal system that provided no protection for women from rape or domestic violence.[24]

In societies that are structured by gender, class, race, religion and sexuality, the more forms of discrimination people suffer, the better they are able to understand how their oppressors think, so they're better able to critique their oppressor's thinking. Thus, the people at the bottom of the social hierarchy – say, women of colour – are best able to help everyone else understand what needs to be done to sort out inequality. When women of colour are lifted out of discrimination, they lift everyone else above them out of discrimination too.[25]

- **treat all people as individuals, don't stereotype**

So, having asked you to trust what I as a white man say, I trust you won't object when I share what many people of colour write about what they experience. Problems arise when people stereotype anyone they have come to look down on. For example, my parked car was once hit by the car of a white man who was backing it out of his driveway. Should I therefore act as if all white men are bad drivers? No, I treat each white man individually and make a judgement after I've observed their driving in the context of their lifestyle over a longer period of time.

If I agree to treat all white men individually rather than stereotyping all white men as the same, then I should also treat people of colour or anyone else individually, too. I trust you'll take this white man's views and the views of people of colour as being equally valid and of equal value.

- **learn from people who are different from you**

Life changed for me when I began work as a community worker in Tooting, inner south London, in 2000. Three-quarters of people in Tooting were postmodern (born from 1961 onwards). About 45 per cent were people of colour.

Modern, middle-class white men like me only formed 2 per cent of the population. No more modern people were being born. I was a dinosaur. Did I, from my culture, have the answers to these people's issues? No.

If I was to be effective in my community work, I had to learn what was important to people who were different from me. Fast. I had to learn what life looked like from other people's points of view. To do that I had to read the books people from their backgrounds had written.

- **respect other people's cultures rather than see your culture as superior**

A traditionally accepted view in the West is that if a white man says something it is right everywhere. This is the principle of universalism: that some ideas apply to everyone universally.[26] What is being implied is, 'Do things our way or go somewhere else.' For people with a different culture the implication is that white people think that the cultures of people of colour are inferior to white people's cultures, and that people of colour need to drop their own culture and copy a white person's culture.

White people will say people of colour need to integrate (get along with white people) but in fact white people mean that people of colour should assimilate (do things the white person's way and drop their own culture). Saying integrate but meaning assimilate is an example of white people's rhetorical ethic: saying one thing and really meaning something else.[27] For example, a doctor might say they are motivated by concern for others, when really they're motivated by a high salary. Many people of colour see this disrespect of their culture as white people's cultural imperialism.

- **learn from people who understand issues better than you do**

Writers with heritage in different continents should, in the view of many, be expected to be experts on those continents, owing to their cultural understanding, rather than white people.[28] Therefore, people should learn from them, that is, people should practise interculturalism.

Interculturalism means to discuss, for example, from a majority-world indigenous person's view of the world with someone having a European's view of the world.[29] Put another way, it is living in a world where different worlds exist together. For example, Mahmood Mamdani has shown his expertise in understanding the causes of conflicts and ways forward in Afghanistan, Iraq and Darfur.[30] Natreema Asafu-Adjaye says of her first trip to Ghana:

'My view of Africa was influenced by the images I had seen on British TV since infancy. The portrayal of famine, disease, impoverished people who resided in shanty towns and mud huts with straw roofs and no electricity and clean water supply.... I remember how surprised I was by the size of the large bungalow-style houses which were more than three times bigger than most terraced properties in Britain. [It] didn't look like the depiction of Africa I'd watch at home on TV.'[31]

'What's next?'

To find out what's really going on in the world and how to best make a difference, white people need to read what people of colour, especially women of colour, write.

This book is in three parts.

Part 1 discusses racism's effect on people of colour. It does so through analyses of race, racism and two of racism's presentations: structural racism and microaggressions.

Part 2 is racism's effect on people who are racist. Having discovered the reality of structural racism, white people need to start learning from people of colour how the world looks to them. This will help white people develop a white anti-racist identity – like learning about everything from scratch again - and start acting as a white person in coalition with people of colour to make a difference. White people discover their whiteness and how the ruling class has distorted their history daily through the media, so that they blamed people of colour for their troubles rather than the ruling class.

Transiting out of Part 2 there's an analysis of Eurocentrism. If this approach is not relevant in currently diverse classrooms an alternative approach is analysed.

This leads into Part 3, issues in schools. There are suggestions for possible ways forward for educators and teachers as regards 'underachievement', the school-to-prison pipeline and the curriculum.

Part 1.

Racism's effect on people of colour

Chapter One. What is race?

'White children are able to identify their racial identity between the ages of four and six. In contrast, other ethnic groups do not choose dolls that reflect their ethnic group until the age of seven, which is likely to be down to an awareness of the value attached to whiteness rather than a reflection of their own racial awareness' (Choudry, 2021).[32]

Some changes in how people have understood race and racism over time.[33]

The Portuguese were the first to treat African people as inferior by only enslaving Africans. The occasion was the landing and sale of 235 enslaved Africans in Lagos, Portugal in 1444, for work as domestic slaves.[34] The enslavement of only Africans resulted from the construction of forts by Eastern Mediterranean Slavic communities to stop slave traders seizing and enslaving their people.[35]

Race appears in a different form in the 1480s[36] in Spain, when the province of Castile established the Inquisition to monitor charges of heresy among Jewish converts to Christianity. Spanish Christians suspected Jewish converts of secretly practising Judaism. The Inquisition was meant to ensure that only 'true Christians' were appointed to central and local government jobs rather than Jews who claimed to have become Christians. To do this the Inquisition checked the 'purity of blood' of applicants' ancestors with people from their home communities who knew of their grandparents. This was a kind of theological race.

When the Spanish invaded Latin America they met people who seemed to them to have no faith: indigenous people and Africans. They set up separate republics for Spanish and indigenous people, carried out 'purity of blood' checks as in Europe and controlled

Africans with laws restricting their freedoms. Since this system depended largely on what people looked like this was an example of colour-coded race, as with Africans in Portugal.

Note that only white people perpetuate racism.[37] By the 19th century, white people saw race as a way to distinguish people by biological category. They used these categories to explain visible differences between people of different cultures and especially to show European superiority.[38] They alleged, for example, that Africans' head shapes showed that they were inferior to white people and that intermarriage between African and white people would cause racial contamination. African writers have been challenging and rejecting these and other allegations for the last 250 years.[39]

However, today, if you compare the DNA of two unrelated people, they are 99.9 per cent identical. This shows that members of the human race are all in some way related to one another and that there are no separate races.[40]

Human life began in Africa in tropical conditions, in which heavily pigmented skin, rich in melanin, gave protection against ultraviolet radiation damage to DNA. When people migrate from the equator, skin colour takes between 10,000 and 20,000 years to adapt to a new latitude. In other words, skin colour just shows how long a person's ancestors have been living away from the equator. Skin colour therefore has nothing at all to do with people's culture, civilisation, characteristics or any supposed superiority or inferiority.[41]

What is race?

'So, you're saying there are no such things as biological races?'

That's right! Race has no scientific or biological validity.[42] But white people have for up to 580 years benefitted financially from their domination of people of colour based on race, and are keeping race alive today for their own financial benefit. Race is what is called a social construct, a value assigned to something based on a collective decision within a society, rather than on a natural or independent existence.[43] I'll explain.

People have opinions about life and see the world through the lens of those opinions. A great deal of knowledge exists only because people give it meaning. Many things in the world are not real but a society gives them meaning by agreeing to that meaning.

For example, cash is pieces of paper and metal that have no value in themselves. Society agrees that these particular pieces of paper and metal are money and everyone then treats them as money.[44] In this way, white is also a social construct. White, defining Europeans as white people, was invented to show which people are considered to be white people, that is, the superior people.

So today it is white people's society that invents the categories of races, and society manipulates or retires these races when convenient.[45] So today race is not about some fixed, or objective social and physical characteristics, but rather race is about relationships of domination and subordination, about power, about the 'haves' and the 'must-not-haves.'[46] So, race *'continues to be the problem of the twenty-first century'*.[47]

Definition of race (socially constructed)

[A] distinct biological type of human being, usually based on their skin colour or other physical characteristics.[48]

How people in universities understand race

'It's really all about class isn't it, not race?'

Academics in universities have largely abandoned using race as an important organisational category. For Marxists, the only action for liberation is class-based. For Marxists, race is on the edge of society rather than at society's centre. Europeans created race as a way to oppress people under capitalism so as to dominate different groups.[49] Marxists discourage workers from organising according to racial solidarity but focus instead on workers of the world uniting together.[50] Marxists see no justifiable basis for race today; for them if you see race you are being racist.

For liberals, society's attitudes have changed fundamentally since enslavement. Liberals feel that people have progressed from a time of ignorance, when they thought racial status signified meaningful difference between people. People have progressed to enlightenment in which race is not seen to make a difference and people have progressed beyond race consciousness. White people aim for people of colour to be integrated with the majority. Many people of colour see this integration as assimilation into white culture and values and hence as losing their own culture and values.[51]

Social domination, whether by race, gender, religion or sexual preference, from the liberal point of view, represents bias and this form of domination should be dealt with similarly.[52] From the liberal perspective, these inequalities are the same in nature. Thus, in Britain, the Commission for Racial Equality was closed down and then incorporated into the Equality and Human Rights Commission. This shows how the state views inequalities. All that is needed is to identify the individuals in society who are overtly physically or verbally racist and just target them.[53]

So, for liberals, seeing racial differences is returning to a backward age, which people need to progress from.[54] For liberals, as with Marxists, to see race is to be racist. The enlightened race-related response for a liberal is to have a colour-blind attitude.[55]

One response to both Marxists and liberals is to engage about examples of structural racism that people of colour are still going through today.[56]

To determine whether some issue is about race, here are three guidelines:

'It is about race if a person of colour thinks it is about race.' People of colour bring their racial identity and also their history of being a person of colour into their experience of all situations.

'It is about race if it disproportionately or differently affects people of colour.' Even though there are a few people of colour who are financially successful, when you take people of colour as a whole, they have measurably poorer outcomes based on race.

'It is about race if it fits into a broader pattern of events that disproportionately or differently affect people of colour.' Being a person of colour in a white-dominated society is often as if you're in an abusive relationship with the world. It's as if you're walking along and someone punches you in the arm. And then another punch. And people punch you in the arm repeatedly. And if you complain people focus only on the last punch and say, 'It's only a small one. I'm sure there was a reason for it. Everyone gets hurt occasionally.'[57]

'But if there's no scientific basis for race, must this be a post-race society?'

First, race is not the parent of racism: racism is the parent of race. Racial discrimination in the form of racist policies comes first, followed by racist ideas, then ignorance and hate.[58]

So, getting rid of the child, race, does not get rid of the parent, racism. And people still then have to engage with racism, which is about white people demonstrating that they are superior to people of colour, based on their colour of skin.[59]

Again, white people set up race so that in an exploitative economic system there's always more profit for white people, who are considered superior, than for people of colour, whose purpose in life is to get less of the profit. This premise, for white people to get more because people of colour are to get less, has been built into all social institutions as structural racism. Since white people have the power to enforce racism it's in white people's interests to keep racism going permanently.[60]

Also, the election of Barack Obama, the first black US President, was the supposed sign of a post-racial age arriving. However, Obama suffered 400 times as many death threats as his predecessor, President George Bush.[61]

CHAPTER TWO. WHAT IS RACISM?

'I was safe at home... until my first day at school when I was released into the gauntlet of the playground. Each day I faced the challenge of rebuilding the little hope and self-esteem that was demolished by the self-hating prejudiced children who were being taught such views by their parents and guardians.... Some of my peers antagonised me about my African ancestry and dark skin complexion.... No matter how much I tried to hide in the corner of the playground or crouch inside the cupboard of the class cloakroom. There was nothing that could deter them from bullying me.... They rejected me because of how I looked. To my peers, dark skin, tough hair and broad features meant that you were ugly, impoverished and uncivilized. I know this is what they believed because they told me so *every single day*' [emphasis mine] (Natreema Asafu-Adjaye, 2015).[62]

There are three forms of racism: cultural, individual and structural.

Cultural racism

With respect to racism today, 'In the new racism, minorities are not biologically inferior, they are seen as culturally different. Cultural difference becomes a way of assigning blame for exclusion and poverty.'[63]

It is as if cultural and religious differences are embodied in nature... when someone says 'Blacks are good at sport, not so good at school. Chinese are good at maths and make good food. Asians are good at business and love family life. Muslims cannot be trusted: they are aggressive, sexist and, under all those clothes, usually a bit wild-eyed.'[64]

This is cultural racism.[65] Cultural racism occurs when people stereotype people of colour's cultures, values and customs or their nature as permanently inferior.[66]

Definition of racism

Any programme or practice of discrimination, segregation, persecution or mistreatment based on membership of a race or ethnic group.[67]

As to the scope of racism:

'Nor is there a single racism, but multiple racisms: colour racism must be examined together with cultural racism, which includes ethnicity, religion and language. Racism … operates along at least three axes: first, that of (belittling, ed.) stereotyping, hatred and violence; secondly, that of a cycle of disadvantage; and the third the negation and even obliteration of culture, religion or language.'[68]

The first of these axes includes common sense racism and microaggressions, which then become ingrained in the second axis, that is, in the culture of organisations as structural racism.[69]

Racialisation is the process of assigning a racial identity to a group that didn't identify itself in this way.

It's important to distinguish between prejudice and racism. Prejudice occurs when people think they are superior to people of colour. But it is only when people go on to say or do something that shows to others that they discriminate against people of colour because they think themselves superior to people of colour that someone can call these words or actions racism.

Discrimination between vs. discrimination against

There is an important difference between discrimination between and discrimination against.[70] Discrimination between is using a set criterion to categorise difference. People that Europeans met when travelling, e.g. Native Americans[71] and Southern Africans,[72] categorised other people according to their observable characteristics or visible differences. And these people established trade links with the Europeans, but did not discriminate against them.

Racism is based on discriminating against. Discriminating against is to place the people you meet into a social system based on their status or authority where that depends on their observable characteristics, and to show that people like yourself are superior to them. Europeans discriminated against many people they met by inflicting on them enslavement, colonialism and genocide.

One of the issues when Europeans categorise people is that Europeans often do not view people as individuals but rather as representatives of social groups. This can lead to tragedies when people make decisions based on stereotypes of a person's group membership. We have been addressing this point about conscious or explicit bias, where people act based on what they consciously decide to do. However, with unconscious or implicit bias, people react in the heat of the moment based on their unconscious thinking, which has been produced by social conditioning and with which their conscious thinking often struggles.[73]

Europeans, then, often think they are right about everything, so that 'because the West got it wrong on race, the concept itself must be wrong and not the Western interpretation. The Western understanding of race is certainly the dominant one, but that does not make it the correct one.' [74]

When a person categorises someone as, for example, a black Muslim woman, Raifa Rafiq, and others, will challenge the associated stereotypes and racial hierarchies that they bring into this situation.

'I am Raifa.... I am a trainee lawyer at one of the best law firms in the world... a writer.... I talk about my amazing podcast and fierce feminism. I do not simply say, "I am a Black Muslim Woman." But this is what others say of me, and in pre-empting the identity that the world gives me, I have internalized it. I am all of these things, but my identity is the intangible part of me that is multifaceted, multidimensional and complex.'[75]

Intersectionality: when your life is shaped by other oppressions in addition to racism

In a majority-white country, it is understandable that it is white men primarily who pass laws according to their agenda. In 1989, the lawyer Kimberle Crenshaw identified that in US, as to employment law, a person could get a positive judgment and justice in one of two ways. Either if they claimed racial discrimination and were an (advantaged) black man. Or if they claimed sexual discrimination and were an (advantaged) white woman.

If, however, instead a person claimed discrimination as a black woman they could get neither a sexual nor a racial discrimination judgment in their favour. This was because black women were not seen as advantaged but for their racial or sexual characteristics in the same way as black men and white women were. White men felt black women were wanting two bites at the discrimination cherry, which they saw as unfair, so they wouldn't give any judgment in black women's favour.

Crenshaw coined the word intersectionality to explain the multiple dimensions of black women's experiences, the experience of which is greater than the sum of race and gender.[76] People's lives can be affected by a number of additional axes of social division, e.g., class, sexuality, ability, citizenship status, Islamophobia, etc.

Further, who is advantaged and disadvantaged in social interactions tells us about the different types of power relations that are operating. People can then start to use these axes of social division to analyse and understand social inequality in an event that people around us face, such as the Grenfell fire of 2017. [77]

Individual racism

Individual racism develops from individual prejudice. Individual racism involves discrimination in a person's relationships with people, whether known or unknown, that they meet informally on the street or in shops.[78]

Individual racism includes microaggressions and everyday[79] racism. A person might profess equality but unconsciously they make an offensive comment. These comments are known as microaggressions.[80] Microaggressions might not sound important but they can have explosive effects.

Microaggressions are everyday exchanges that send insulting messages to people because of the group they are seen as being a member of.[81] While the speaker's intention might be positive and to compliment someone, the other person is left with a bad feeling and a range of physical and mental health problems, while stereotypes are reinforced for both speaker and listener.[82]

Common comments made, or racial microaggressions

'I don't see colour.'

White people are afraid that anything they say might appear racist. One way in which they avoid a conversation is to deny that they see colour. This is to emphasise what people have in common rather than their differences. But saying they don't see colour makes people of colour suspicious that white people are trying to cover up their racial biases. That although white people might feel they are being progressive by saying they're colour blind, in reality those white people are being evasive.[83]

'I don't see colour' is based on the idea that the colour black itself is a negative. However, what's really negative are the associations that have been forced on the meaning of the colour black.[84] So, in the *Oxford English Dictionary* (1989) most meanings of the word 'black' are negative, grouped under the categories dirt, emotion, death, evil and immoral. In the same dictionary most connotations of the word 'white' are positive, grouped into the categories of cleanliness, things favoured and legitimate, and turning bad into good.[85]

The word 'black' started gaining negative connotations in the Middle Ages, which was probably to do with the Crusades. The explosion of negative connotations in the 16th century probably tied in with the beginnings, at least for English speakers, of European adventures in imperialism and colonialism.[86]

'When people proudly tell me that, when it comes to race, they are colour blind, I want to shake them and remind them that blindness is a disability.'[87] 'By saying they don't see colour, white people are erasing people of colour's everyday experience of racism.'[88]

Colour blindness was started by Republicans in the US to stop civil rights laws. It moved from the US government to the British government during the 1980s. Colour-blind ideology is today government policy on racial inequality not only in the US and UK, but also widely in Europe, the Caribbean and Latin America, and is widely believed by many ordinary people in those societies.[89]

The logic of colour blindness, when faced with claims of racist inequalities, goes as follows. Most people believe in racial equality and the laws have been changed to outlaw discrimination. I don't see colour (so I can't be racist). Since no special benefits accrue to me based on whiteness (see Chapter 3), racism isn't causing these inequalities. If all of these assumptions are true (some might say, 'If I've passed my own litmus test'), the reason these inequalities are happening is because of individual weaknesses and behaviour. That's a lot of conditions to pass![90]

Here it is necessary to pause the conversation on microaggressions to look at how structural racism is a major challenge to this argument about being colour blind.

CHAPTER THREE. 'THEY'VE GOT EQUALITY – WHAT ARE THEY COMPLAINING ABOUT?'

'Did they teach you that words that just slip out of your mouth, or behaviour you're barely aware of, can tap into and reinforce a system of structural racism and white supremacy that dates back centuries? Probably not. And no, that's not your fault. We can only know what we're taught, or experience ourselves. I don't need to read a book or sit a course on oppression; I've lived it *every day of my life*' (emphasis mine) (Sheri Carr, 2017).[91]

Structural racism

Structural racism distorts equal opportunity. So, people who say they're colour blind and that people all progress on merit are ignoring the fact that meritocracy works in white people's favour and against people of colour. Analyses of structural racism show what an average black boy may face as he seeks to make his way in Britain.[92]

Structural racism is a form of racism expressed in the practice of social and political institutions. It is reflected in disparities in, for example, wealth, income, criminal justice, employment, housing, health care, political power and education. The black boy and his parents might have high hopes, but from the time they begin school, black boys have the odds against them.[93]

Education

Black Caribbean pupils start off well. At age five they are hardly at all (3 per cent) below the average of all English pupils for a good level of development.[94] However, when they take SATS at age 11, many of their own teachers will systematically mark black Caribbeans, black Africans, Pakistanis and Bangladeshis down.[95]

Black Caribbean and mixed white/Caribbean pupils are each around two and a half times more likely to be excluded permanently compared with white British pupils. However, in Harrow, Brent and Haringey London boroughs, black Caribbean pupils are five times more likely than white British pupils to be excluded. Historically, 10 per cent of schools make nearly 90 per cent of these exclusions. Some academy chains exclude pupils at high rates in order to enforce uniform policies.[96]

Police assumptions about black boys' gang affiliations may be encouraging knife crime against black boys

The Metropolitan Police has assumed that black boys tend to be affiliated with gangs. In 2012 they set up a 'gangs violence matrix' to measure the likelihood of violence from London's 'known gang members'. By 2016, 78 per cent of those on this matrix were black, 13 per cent white and 9 per cent from other groups. The Met was alleging that black boys were disproportionately likely to be gang members.

A report by Amnesty International considered that indicators the police used to identify gang members did not relate to serious crime. It said police were operating using prejudiced stereotypes.[97] Since police stereotype black boys as likely gang members it is not surprising that young people are stereotyping any black boys as gang members and killing them.

In England and Wales, from 2016 to 2017 and 2019 to 2020, the homicide rate was 49.5 per million population for black people, about five times higher than for white people (9.4 per million population) and four times higher than for other ethnicities. Around half of homicides of black people were of those aged 16 to 24.[98]

People living in poverty are more likely to get involved in crime outside school. The disproportionate number of child victims of homicide correlates with the finding that black people are the broad ethnic group that is most likely to live in the most income-deprived 10 per cent of neighbourhoods in England.[99]

Higher education

Later, black pupils are less likely to be accepted into the prestigious Russell Group of universities than their white peers.[100] If they make it to university, like many others, the black pupil will want a 2 i or 1st – a 'good' degree. However, in 2019/20, while 85.9 per cent of white pupils were awarded a 'good' degree, only 65.8 per cent of black pupils achieved this, an attainment gap of 20.1 per cent.[101] Black pupils were the group most likely to have the lowest-ranking results – 2 ii, 3rd or a pass.

Employment

When it comes to applying for jobs, a black boy might not feel there is much chance of building a career in higher education since 90 per cent of professors are white.[102] Researchers have found that job applicants with names that sound white are interviewed far more often than applicants with names sounding like people of colour.[103]

Further, from 1991 to 2011 black Caribbean and African younger men have had unemployment rates more than double those of white men.[104] In mid-2014, more than one in four of all black 18 to 24-year-olds were out of work.[105]

Criminal justice system

With respect to the criminal justice system, in the year 2019 to 2020, black people were nine times more likely to be stopped and searched than white people. The Met Police in London carried out 49 per cent of all stops and searches in England and Wales, and made 80 per cent of all searches of black people in England and Wales.[106]

Black men are over three times more likely to be arrested than white men.[107]

Covid-19

In April 2020, 27 per cent of black ethnic groups reported finding it quite difficult or very difficult to cope financially, compared with

8 per cent of Indian, 7 per cent of white British and 13 per cent of Pakistani and Bangladeshi backgrounds. This is because black people were less likely to have enough financial assets to cover a drop in income. This reflected their working in insecure and poorly paid jobs.

Once lockdown began people of colour were more likely to be working longer hours, but less likely to be employed and less eligible for furlough than white people. Because they were working at their workplace rather than from home, when protective equipment was less available, they were more exposed to Covid-19 and so more likely to die.

At the beginning of the first lockdown, 36 per cent of Indian people and 35 per cent of black people reported that they were persistently losing sleep over worry, compared with 23 per cent of white people. This shows that the mental well-being of Indian and black people may have been significantly affected by Covid-19.[108]

Some results of recognising structural racism

Many white people see racism as an issue for each individual person, so they fail to see collective action that results in and maintains structural racism. Meanwhile, white supremacy tells white people that the problems of people of colour stem from their own failures, so white people are not guilty or responsible for racism. So white people feel they are innocent of racism, while at the same time they collaborate in maintaining structural racism and benefitting daily from it.[109]

People of colour are locked into a global capitalist system that racism is an integral part of. People of colour worldwide exist to provide goods cheaply so that people in the West can have an easy life.[110]

Discrimination leads to poverty. Racial discrimination is the only cause of racial inequality worldwide.[111]

People of colour say that people wanting to stop racism need to focus on stopping structural racism rather than on stopping individual racism. Lindsay sees racism as like an iceberg. People easily see individual acts of racism, but it's important to focus efforts on destroying the majority of racism, that is, structural racism, the underwater majority of the iceberg, which to many people's sight is 'just not there'.[112]

They say they're colour blind, but their actions show they don't practice colour blindness

Eddo-Lodge says that colour blindness is equivalent to enforced assimilation, with her blackness being ignored in the attempt to gain false harmony. The drastic differences in life chances resulting from structural racism against black boys show that, while social institutions say they are colour blind, they don't practise colour blindness.

Kimberle Crenshaw told her that colour blindness implies that to get rid of race you have to get rid of all discussion about race, including the acknowledgement of racial hierarchies and doing something about them.

Eddo-Lodge says that colour blindness only gets as far as saying people shouldn't discriminate against someone because of the colour of their skin. Colour blindness does not engage with the ways structural dominant power often shows itself in white–black encounters. When people of colour try to explain the racism they experience, people who believe in colour blindness often accuse people of colour of being racist against white people. This enables believers in colour blindness to continue to deny white people's accountability.

People of colour's resulting enforced silence about telling the truth about racism makes people of colour feel they are aliens in the country they were born in. Telling yourself and your children that people are all equal denies the legacy of a British society that has been organised since the 18th century by race.[113] Saying people are all equal is a social construct that maintains racial domination and injustice.

White children are taught not to 'see race', while the children of many people of colour are taught that they need to be twice as good as white children to succeed. Being colour blind doesn't deconstruct racist structures or improve people of colour's daily conditions.

To dismantle race, people have to see race. To see who benefits from race, who gets impacted by negative stereotypes about race, and who gets power and advantage owing to their gender, race and class. People have to see race to change the system.[114]

Helping racism's perpetrators change their ways

Stopping sexism is primarily about sorting out men and their problem behaviour. So, stopping racism is primarily about sorting out white people and their problem behaviour. A programme on Instagram challenges white people to a one-month daily check-up on aspects of white people's actions and behaviour, such as:

You and white fragility (how you might feel when someone brings up the issue of racism)

You and white silence (keeping quiet about racism)

You and white saviourism (thinking white people have the answers to people of colour's problems)[115]

Here are two of these actions:

White supremacy

Structural racism shows that racism is not solely a subjective experience, but an objective structural force.[116] 'White supremacy is the unnamed political system that has made the world what it is today.'[117]

This white supremacy doesn't mean only the obvious racism of white supremacist groups such as the Ku Klux Klan. Rather, it refers to an economic, political and cultural system.

'A system in which white people control both power and also material resources. In which, both consciously and unconsciously, ideas and thoughts about white superiority and white entitlement are everywhere. And in which relationships between white people who are dominant and people of colour who are subordinate are acted out every day across a broad range of social settings and institutions.'[118]

White supremacy results in white people stopping people of colour from achieving their goals in life. This results in people of colour feeling powerless. Acts of violence are done by powerless people who want to gain their self-esteem and demonstrate their significance. Because young people of colour feel they cannot be violent towards white people they are tempted to turn their violence against other young people of colour.[119]

White supremacy is the way in which a society organises itself, based on the belief that whites are valued more than everyone else. This is the 'value gap', which is seen as part of the country's DNA. Stopping racism requires people to value everyone else as much as they value themselves.[120]

White structurally embedded advantage[121]

Part of the common sense that the ruling class have handed down to today is that, because people have an equality of opportunity in Britain, they can all achieve as much financially as the amount of hard work they're willing to put in. Those who then don't put in much effort become poor and are seen as undeserving of receiving an acceptable amount of social security.

The reality that people found during the run-up to the Brexit referendum was that white people were saying that the white poor were actually deserving while the undeserving ones were immigrants and people of colour. This recognition by white people that the poorest white person was deserving of an acceptable amount of social security reflects white people's understanding that every white person is advantaged above people of colour.[122]

White structurally embedded advantage is that if you're white your life will be positively impacted by being part of the white racial group at least once and possibly every day. Probably without you ever being aware of it.[123]

Try this exercise exploring the existence of white structurally embedded advantage in Britain. Look at race on its own, ignoring other identities that could affect the result. If you believe the statement is usually true, score 0. If it's sometimes true, score 3. If it's false, score 5.

'If ever I am stopped by the police, I would feel that it is likely they singled me out because of my skin colour.'

'From nursery to this day, the teachers I have had don't share the same skin colour as me.'

'People online or in public have directed racist slurs at me.'

'When I am told about national heritage, about human history or about civilisation, I am shown people who do not share the same culture or skin colour as me.'

'Whenever I ask to speak to "the person in charge", I can be sure I will be facing someone who does not have the same skin colour as me.'[124]

Add up your score. Divide your total score by 25 and multiply it by 100 to get the total amount of white structurally embedded advantage that you benefit from. 100 is the score of people who benefit most from white structurally embedded advantage. Nought is the score of people who benefit least from white structurally embedded advantage. Ask someone of a different racial background to complete the test. Then compare the results. Discuss insights you both gained from the process.

Further, if people are going to consider white structurally embedded advantage, they need to look at it from the perspective of oppressed people of colour rather than from the perspective of white people. They then also need to consider the ongoing white supremacy of white British people expressed in acts of white domination that are worldwide because of the extent of the British Empire, therefore part of British history. These acts, which people can list, may have been in the past but they are linked to the present through neo-colonialism and coloniality since independence.[125]

Neo-colonialism is the use today of capitalism, cultural imperialism and conditional aid to direct the political and economic policies of other countries. It uses foreign capital to exploit rather than develop less-developed countries. Neo-colonialism is a lever of global coloniality.[126]

Coloniality, or the colonial matrix of power, is a global system with three main aspects, led by the US and its NATO partners, especially their ruling classes. It says that social power is dependent on skin colour, with light-skinned being most desirable and dark-skinned least desirable. It is Eurocentric, indicating that countries wishing to advance need to copy the ways that European countries became nation states. Finally, it says that Europeans are the best source of knowledge in everything.[127]

CHAPTER FOUR. 'WHAT ARE MICROAGGRESSIONS?'

'I started getting loads of comments about me being black. Meat ones like calling me a burnt chicken nugget and the N-word and saying I've got privileges because I'm black and it hasn't really been sorted out. It's been getting worse for the past three weeks, calling me stuff like I should be kicked out of school and it makes me feel kind of sad because I've just been trying to make friends' (Ashley Davies, 11-year-old, after he moved to Cornwall from Liverpool, 2019).[128]

'But people of colour are racist towards white people, aren't they?' Reverse racism

What people of colour hear in this question is that the oppression they feel daily is a delusion.[129]

Prejudice is real among communities of colour. Prejudice is unreasonable feelings, opinions or attitudes, especially of a hostile nature, directed against a racial, religious or national group.[130] An unattributed definition of racism defines it as prejudice plus power. But black people don't have enough people in powerful positions to perform racism towards white people on the scale that white people currently operate racism against black people.[131]

Here is an example of prejudice without power. If I, a white man, go into an African-Caribbean café to get a takeaway for an African-Caribbean friend, I might not get as good food as people of colour. But that's as far as the prejudice will go in a majority-white society. It's like the action of a trickster (an oppressed person who uses skills they're especially good at to outwit an oppressor).[132] I can get away from that prejudice by not shopping in that shop, or by moving out of the area. But for racism, in the form of prejudice plus power, look at any of the examples of structural racism above. People of colour can't get away from that situation anywhere in Britain.[133]

'If people just stop talking about it [racism] it will go away.'

Apparently, Morgan Freeman agrees with this.[134] But what if engineers and scientists thought this way, believing that the best way of solving a problem was not to challenge the problem but to leave it alone and hope it worked itself out? There would not have been any progress ever if people had not decided to challenge difficult problems with discussion and then action.[135]

'Where are you from? No, where are you really from?'

What people of colour hear in these questions is that they don't belong as citizens in the place where they are asked these questions. Instead, they hear that their allegiance rests with another country, which by implication they ought to go back to if they complain about conditions in this country.[136]

'Stop playing the race card.'

Many people see racism as a type of card that people can play, rather like a joker. So, it's a card that's versatile and can be used in any situation. Only people of colour play this card so as to say sorry for their personal failings – even those people of colour who are successful materially. Akala says that people racialised as white are unable to play this race card, in the same way that they can't be terrorists. So, the action of European empires in colonising most of the planet has not had any effect towards shaping human history; it's just been people of colour playing cards.

But people of colour who speak about racial exclusion do not ask for special treatment. Rather, they are challenging why special, structurally embedded advantages should be given to the dominant, white group.[137]

David Starkey's comments on the 2011 riots indicate that when whites looted, they did so, in his opinion, as a result of Jamaican influence on white culture, as a result of which he said, 'The whites have become black.' Speaking of David Lammy, Starkey went on to say, 'Archetypal, successful black man. If you turn the screen off so that you are listening to him on radio you would think he was white.'[138]

Starkey is thereby implying that if black people want to be successful, they should aspire to become like white people. The message of both Starkey's points is black negative, white positive. Starkey shows that it is allowed for someone to say the word 'black', but only if they are a white person, as a result of which that white person is not silenced for 'playing the race card'.[139]

'Why can't you just get over it? It's all in the past. It's time to move on.'

This statement implies that history is not something for people to learn from, but rather that it's a big boulder for people to get over. But people aren't trying to get over Plato, Leonardo da Vinci or Shakespeare.

It's odd that in a country where many people are proud of the British Empire, that anyone criticising one of its obvious legacies should be told to get over it, when the Empire is something that white people are proud of. If people were to 'get over' – or forget – the past, would people have to become hunter-gatherers and farmers all over again? At what point in history would people be allowed to start remembering from? In reality they don't want to have conversations they might find uncomfortable.[140]

'Slavery did not cause the [British, ed.] Industrial Revolution, but played an active role in its pattern and timing.'[141]

People of colour cannot escape the enduring effects of slavery today, reflecting on the results, for example, of 46,000 British families in 1833 making compensation claims for losing emancipated slaves.[142]

David Cameron famously said, 'I do hope that … we can move on from this painful legacy' when challenged to give reparations for slavery in Jamaica.[143] It's not surprising that he said this. Cameron's first cousin six times removed, General Sir James Duff, was awarded £4,101 – more than £3 million in today's money – as compensation for 202 slaves that he forfeited on Jamaica's Grange sugar estate. Further, Susannah Cameron is related to William Jolliffe, who received £4,000 in compensation for 164 slaves freed on an estate he owned in St Lucia.[144]

British taxpayers paid compensation to claimants totalling £20 million – £17 billion in today's money – or 40 per cent of the government's annual expenditure at that time. This was the largest British government payout until the 2009 bailout of the banks, being effectively a payout by British taxpayers to many of today's ruling class in Britain.[145] The loan that the government borrowed to pay the slave owners was not fully repaid until 2015. So not only I but millions of others including people of colour have been paying taxes all of their lives to compensate former rich slave owners.[146]

'You have a chip on your shoulder.'

People can't define what having a chip on a shoulder means, although people know black boys, especially, seem to have them. People with big chips on their shoulders include Muhammad Ali and Colin Kaepernick. These are men who gave up millions of dollars to protest about injustice. They could have kept quiet about injustice and continued bringing in the millions. But not when their political opponents were in favour of bombing Vietnam in one case, and trying to ignore US police brutality in killing unarmed black people in the other.[147]

'Why don't you just go back to where you came from?'

Akala was born in London, so born in Britain like many of his peers. If he were to go to Jamaica the lightness of his skin would result in him being treated as upper-class. He wouldn't face violence or police harassment there. He would have better material conditions than the poorest people in Britain, so would not have any need to live off food banks or freeze due to homelessness in winter.[148]

'But didn't colonialism leave some positive legacies, like hospitals in Africa and railways in India?'

A YouGov poll in 2014 showed that 59 per cent of British people saw the British Empire as 'something to be proud of', while 49 per cent felt the Empire benefitted the colonies.[149]

The Sub-Saharan African colony situation is complicated. One way to compare colony experiences is to put them into three categories: those with a centralised pre-colonial state in 1885 when the Scramble for Africa took place; those where significant white settlement took place; and all the other colonies.

After an extensive review of the data, literature and arguments, Heldring and Robinson found in the first two categories clear evidence that colonialism retarded development. In the third category, they found that while colonies were of different types and that their colonial experience was more ambiguous. It would be difficult to come up with scenarios under which colonialism promoted development.

Where railways were constructed, as in Sierra Leone or Ghana, they were positioned to rule not develop the colony. After the Hut Tax Rebellion in Sierra Leone in 1898, the route of the railway was changed so as to control the heart of the rebellion in Mendeland. In a similar way to 19th century southern US medical provision for enslaved Africans,[150] hospitals were built to minimise the likelihood of infectious diseases in Africans spreading to white people.[151] Throughout Nigeria in the 1930s, the 4,000 Europeans in the colony had 12 modern hospitals, while the 40 million Africans had just 52 hospitals.[152]

Africa was very poor in 1885 compared with the rest of the world. India, however, had one of the strongest economies in 1757, at the beginning of British rule. Yet between 1757 and 1947 there was no increase in income per head on the Indian subcontinent. The railways are often cited as a positive legacy of colonialism but they were built to transport troops inland to quell revolts, as well as to move food out of productive areas for export, including in times of famine. So, during the famines of 1876–8 and 1896–1900, when between 12 and 30 million Indians died of hunger, death rates were highest in those areas serviced by British railways.[153]

'You should be grateful that you have free speech.'

Britain has a long history of suppressing people's speech. Free speech in Britain resulted from hard-won freedoms through the sacrifices of the Chartists. It was not granted by enlightened leaders.[154] Although born in London, Akala says that Jamaica, where one of his parents is from, was ranked eighth in the world in 2017 for press freedom, while Britain, where his other parent is from, was down at number 40. If press freedom exists in politically challenging Jamaica, what exactly should people be grateful for in the sixth richest nation of the world? [155]

Part 2.

Racism's effect on people who are racist

Chapter Five. 'How can I develop a positive white identity?'

(Speaking about white American authors appearing to ignore African people's presence in the US). 'Another reason for this… is the pattern of thinking about racialism in terms of its consequences on the victim… the object of racist policy and attitudes.... [T]hat well-established study should be joined with another, equally important one: the impact of racism on those who perpetuate it…. My project is an effort to avert the critical gaze from the racial object to the racial subject; from the described and imagined to the describers and imaginers; from the serving to the served' (Toni Morrison, 1992).[156]

Introduction

Beverly Tatum often asks people who attend her workshops, 'What is your class and ethnic background?' White people wonder what to call themselves ethnically. One woman said, 'I'm just normal'! But if she was normal, are people different from her 'just abnormal?' Because in a majority-white society, whiteness is the unexamined norm and many white people think that racial identity is something other people have, so it's not relevant to them.

Whiteness can be defined as, 'the impact of racism on those who perpetuate it', as Toni Morrison says above. 'But I'm not racist.' In response, Kendi says:

'The opposite of "racist" isn't "not racist". The opposite of racist is antiracist.... Racist policies lead to racial inequity and injustice, while antiracist policies lead to racial equity, and justice.... [W]hen you do nothing in the face of the status quo, what happens to the status quo? It stays the same, right? So to do nothing in the face of racism is to be racist, is to allow racism to persist. Because the only way racism will be eliminated is if we challenge it.'[157]

In a race-conscious society, the messages people receive about superiority and inferiority shape how they see reality and influence how they interact with others. In that society, the task of people of colour is to resist negative messages and develop an empowered sense of self. White people need to develop a positive white identity based on reality rather than on their superiority.

This requires that white people recognise their whiteness and accept it, in the context of a personal commitment to bringing about a just society. White people's two main developmental tasks in this process are abandoning personal racism and recognising and opposing cultural and structural racism. These tasks take place through six statuses (states of mind): contact, disintegration, reintegration, pseudo-independence, immersion/emersion and autonomy.[158]

Abandoning racism

Many white children when they are young go through a process of being shamed by their parents or peers into accepting the ideas of white supremacy. White children accept white supremacy as a result of those parents or peers threatening to withhold their love from them and treating them as undeserving of being accepted as white people unless they avoid mixing with people of colour.[159]

During their youth, many young white people absorb messages communicated subtly through social conditioning that may go unrecognised and unchallenged for a long time. Peggy McIntosh speaks for many people when she says, 'I was taught to recognise racism only in individual acts of meanness by members of my group, never in invisible systems conferring unsought racial dominance on my group from birth.'

At the contact status, or state of mind, therefore, white people often see themselves as colour blind and free of prejudice. They often deny any historical involvement of their family in racism. They may also see racism as the action of some prejudiced individuals. White people are also often unaware of their white structurally embedded advantage – that is, how white people benefit daily from racism only because of their skin colour and even though they are unaware of it. A few examples of white structurally embedded advantage given by McIntosh are:

'7. When I am told about our national heritage or about "civilization", I am shown that people of my color made it what it is.'

'27. I can go home from most meetings of organisations I belong to feeling somewhat tied in [involved, ed.], rather than isolated, out-of-place, outnumbered, unheard, held at a distance or feared.'

'47. I can travel alone or with my spouse without expecting embarrassment or hostility in those who deal with us.'[160]

Eddo-Lodge says that white structurally embedded advantage is also a way that white people can maintain dominance over people of colour. People of colour need to have conversations with white people about what the consequences of white people's racism are for people of colour. However, the fact that white people are unaware of their structurally embedded advantage means that they may well suspect people of colour of 'reverse racism' against white people.

This conversation, therefore, can put at risk a person of colour's friendships, flat or job and income. White structurally embedded advantage owns the company that recruits you and the money you need to live, so white advantage literally shuts the person of colour up from speaking.[161] In my opinion it is hardly surprising if white advantage has a bad effect on the person of colour's mental health.

In the next status, disintegration, white people become more aware of white structurally embedded advantage and of racism when they see a visible occurrence of racism. This might result from a close relationship with a person of colour.

For example, they may see shop security paying far more attention to a person of colour than to themselves, or checkout or security staff might ask people of colour for more in the way of identification. Or they might become more aware of harsher security restraints on a person of colour or of a death in police custody.

A good way to introduce people to the way in which white people have been racist towards people of colour is for them to watch the film *Ethnic Notions*,[162] which portrays media-driven caricatures, especially of black people in US from 1840 to 1980, in an attempt to justify discrimination against them.

A British equivalent treatment is BBC4's *TimeShift: Black and White Minstrel Show*.[163] An analysis of the caricatures is also available on the Internet.[164]

This awareness of racism brings discomfort. People experience shame, guilt and anger when aware of their own or their family's prejudice. Further, seeing inequalities in society contradicts talk of a meritocracy. If a person continues to be interested in stopping racism, they may challenge racism on TV or from their acquaintances.

However, friends and family will put pressure on people during their disintegration status not to recognise racism, causing the white person to ask themselves whether the costs of challenging racism outweigh the benefits.

Relief from this rejection by friends and family can come from entering the reintegration status. The person reduces their anxiety unfortunately by readopting the view of racism that their friends, family and social conditioning hold. They so regain their support from the white community.

Their previous feelings of guilt or denial get transformed into anger towards people of colour. Their feeling is that if racism is a problem, people of colour's behaviour must have caused the problem. This is blaming the victim.

One thing people learn as they go through McIntosh's 50 examples of white structurally embedded advantage is that white people treat other white people as individuals, whereas white people often tend to treat people of colour as typical of people from their background as a group. For example, McIntosh says.

'18. I can swear, or dress in second hand clothes, or not answer letters, without having people attribute these choices to the bad morals, the poverty or the illiteracy of my race.'

'20. I can do well in a challenging situation without being called a credit to my race.'

'21. I am never asked to speak for all the people of my racial group.'

White people's treatment of people of colour as their being typical of people from their background as a group is done by stereotyping. That is, by producing one-sided descriptions resulting from the collapsing of complex differences to produce a simplistic cardboard cut-out.[165]

Stereotypes are part of the way children and later adults can achieve the illusion of controlling both themselves and their world.[166] Stereotyping gives a person power. Power is the ability not just to tell the story of another person, but to make it the definitive story of that person.[167]

What happens in the reintegration status in this connection is that white people feel that people of colour view white people as members of a group rather than as individuals, which causes the individual white person anger and discomfort. People of colour will test a white person to see whether they respond similarly to other members of the white group in a racist way or whether the white person passes a person of colour's test of their becoming anti-racist.

The fourth status, pseudo-independence, is reached when the white person stops blaming people of colour for their situation and commits themselves to unlearning their own racism. However, having recognised the everyday nature of racism, the white person recognises and experiences their whiteness at this point as a reason for shame.

The fifth status has two aspects, immersion and emersion. Immersion is a search for the meaning of whiteness and racism, to understand the ways in which you benefit from them.[168] It also includes redefining a more positive, humanistic, anti-racist form of whiteness, that of being a white coalition-builder.[169]

It involves people consciously getting rid of the socially conditioned racism that they had operated by before. They thereby end up with an understanding of whiteness that goes beyond being a victimizer to whiteness being a reason for pride.

Emersion is withdrawal into the company of anti-racist white people. This has a number of benefits. This group of similarly-minded people are able to explain issues you face from their journeys. They are able to provide support and keep the individual going in their work. They show that the work of the white coalition-builder is not so much to provide help to victims of racism, but rather to challenge structural racism and challenge other white people to do likewise.

Finding white anti-racist coalition-builders is quite a bit harder to do in Britain than in the US. I would suggest starting by reading books by Americans such as Lois Stalvey, Mab Segrest, Becky Thompson, Tema Okun, Jacqueline Battalora and Debby Irving.[170]

White people are encouraged to work through issues of guilt and shame with anti-racist white people because this is an experience that people of colour find painful when white people go through it with them. Further, this prepares white people for the fact that people of colour will want white people to engage with other white people in future rather than with people of colour.[171]

The final status is autonomy. The person incorporates their newly identified definition of whiteness into their racial identity. This then energises their action to challenge oppression and racism daily. It also enables them to have respectful relationships with people of colour.[172]

Chapter Six. 'What can I do to end racism?'

The suggestion to 'be an ally' has a lot of issues. Like many 19th century abolitionists of slavery, you can still see people of colour as inferior while you work for people to treat them with equality.[173] Further, you may think whiteness only damages people of colour rather than damaging white people as well, so your actions may end up reinforcing whiteness.

Also, you may fail to learn from history that class, capitalism and white supremacy are real issues, while you instead focus on 'getting rid of your white advantage'. Again, people's thinking today is very much determined by social media. So they replace 'doing something' with 'saying something', when they should be replacing charity with solidarity. Finally, a consistent set of demands is replaced by generalised anger.

Coalition-building

Coalition building focusses on identifying shared interests. It builds on the history of black resistance and the black radical tradition. Malcolm X tells white people, 'Work in conjunction with us – each one working with our own kind.'[174] For example, Fred Hampton and Huey P. Newton encouraged working class white people to form white-only groups, list their demands, such as against racism, capitalist inequalities and police brutality and march with people of colour.[175]

Then, when people understand what is meant by race, racism, whiteness and white supremacy they need to remember this is all part of a racist ideology, that these are bad things that everyone needs to destroy. They cannot be allowed to keep people bound in the old structures.[176]

Challenging structural racism – community development groups

Gillborn concludes his analysis of structural racism in education by putting it down to 'a web of actions by teachers, policymakers, right-wing commentators, uncritical academics and the media – all working in one direction, day after day and to incredibly powerful effect.'[177]

Looking more broadly at structural racism throughout US society, Kivel puts structural racism down similarly to 'a web of control'.[178] He's referring to the actions of the ruling class that are put in place by people in the moderate, middle-class mainstream (e.g., journalists, textbook writers and company personnel managers).[179]

People of colour insist that people should prioritise working against structural racism over helping individuals change to an anti-racist identity. To do this, white people need to work together with other like-minded people, rather than on their own. They need to find a community development or activist group that operates in a local area where they can work in an organised way against racism.

Some examples of activist groups in Britain that work against racism include Hope Not Hate; Stand Up To Racism; Rock Against Racism; Black Lives Matter; People's Assembly and Black Activists Rising Against Cuts.

Community development groups are likely to be more successful if the people who facilitate the group are seen to be led by the ordinary members of the community to projects that the ordinary members wish to do. This is a situation in which there is an equality and democracy among the group and its facilitators.

Sadly, in many, perhaps most, community development groups in Britain the facilitators are seen to be those who decide what action needs to be taken and then take the action, while the ordinary members are just there to be led by the facilitators.

Groups can change over time in the way they operate, for example if they operate in a democracy between the facilitators and the ordinary members or in a hierarchy. You might need to try a group in order to see whether, for example, you are happy with the way in which action is decided upon and taken by ordinary members, or you are happy with the way that female voices are valued.[180]

One issue that might come up is whether the community development group is meant only for people of colour or whether white people are free to join. This might seem strange but it reflects the history of white people feeling at liberty to assume they can take over leadership of any organisation they wish, in the same way as white people have used their economic power to impose their system of capitalism on the rest of the world.

This action of white takeover, which imposes a racial hierarchy with whites being superior, has caused many problems in the history of civil rights and often results in white people being asked to work only with other white people.[181]

Alinsky says that in community work, people need to think about and reflect on what is happening. This is so that they can understand what general patterns there are to what the community is doing and experiencing so that they understand better how to go forward with the community. They need to reflect and educate themselves so that they can critique the situation.[182]

White coalition-builders need to recognise that the issues the group are concerned with are in fact the same issues as working-class people across Britain are facing. Recognising the limitations of the resources and influence of their own group it is useful to work together with trade unions and the Labour movement. So as to increase the likelihood of being able to achieve social and political change.[183]

Chapter Seven. 'What is whiteness?'

'White people do not really have to consider how their whiteness is an ever-present non-presence that moulds and shapes a lived reality; which bestows "gifts", "benefits" and "privileges" upon them that have to be "earned", in one way or another, by Black people' (William (Lez) Henry, 2007).[184]

'I came across a documentary entitled *Whitewashed: unmasking the world of whiteness*....[185] The vast majority of participants declared that they have never been challenged to think consciously about their whiteness.... In a westernised society I have been conditioned to factor my blackness into every decision I make' (Natreema Asafu-Ajaye, 2015).[186]

Definition of whiteness

Whiteness is the effect on white people's thinking and action of the racism that they do to people of colour.[187]

Whiteness is a way of thinking that structurally advantages white people. It also assumes white people to be the norm.[188]

Whiteness is a framework that says racism does not exist. It denies the existence of structural racism. It claims that white people's success results from their individual merit and people of colour's failure results from their individual inadequacy.[189]

Whiteness has three linked dimensions:

A place of structurally embedded advantage.

A standpoint from which white people look at themselves, others and the world.

A range of cultural practices that white people both do not notice and make obscure.[190]

The only writing that is credible in areas such as whiteness and racism is that which comes from people of colour, because they have experience of being victims of these and have thereby developed expertise in analysing them. White people, who do not have experience of being victims of racism and as a result cannot see whiteness, are right to acknowledge their indebtedness to the insights of people of colour.[191]

Whiteness is an invisible norm. When white people discuss multiculturalism they are referring to people of colour but do not include white people. Because whiteness is therefore racially unmarked, some white people don't understand how it works daily and white people don't understand what it means to be white. Because white people and whiteness are not, therefore, racialised, whiteness is able to function as an ethnically neutral category. Whiteness can then go unexplored and unchallenged as everyone's standard, as to how people are expected to act and how they are evaluated as people.[192]

The white racial frame

'The better we know our racial past, the better we know our racial present.'[193] White people tend to have in their thinking a white racial frame. Social sciences use the idea of a frame that gives perspective, that gets embedded in people's minds and in people's collective histories and memories, and helps them make sense out of everyday situations.

People are multi-framers and use numerous frames for understanding and interpretation in their minds, with frames varying in complexity from micro-level framing of individual situations to a broad frame of society. The white racial frame is an overarching white world view encompassing a broad 'set of racial stereotypes, prejudices, ideologies, images, interpretations and narratives, emotions, and reactions to language accents, as well as racialised inclinations to discriminate.'

Who's driving white racial framing in Britain?

There are many in majority-white countries who will say that they are being victimised as white people. They will point to people from Central and Eastern Europe or people of colour and say that they are taking the jobs that white British people want to have. That the practice of multiculturalism and diversity tends to work against the employment of white males.[194] In Brexit, many noticed people who had seen their job income and life chances diminished voting Leave to get their voices heard.

In Britain the conceptualisation of these ideas has been spearheaded by the mainstream media, the majority of which is owned by a handful of billionaires and hence tends to have views on the political Right.[195]

For example, the journalist Peter Hitchens has developed the concept of a 'liberal elite'. Through this he criticises people on the Left in the Labour party, who support disadvantaged groups, such as women, LGBTQIA+, people of colour, migrants and poor people pressing for justice and equality. He criticises them as doing away with traditional ways of British life. Hitchens condemns the words and actions of people who support this 'liberal elite' as 'political correctness."[196]

He is really complaining about people being stopped from continuing to exploit and abuse people from these backgrounds. Hitchens is making a case for social conservatism. *The Mail on Sunday* headlines Hitchens' take on the results of the 2011 Census as 'alien nation', where traditional British culture, language, religion, work practices and values seem to be being replaced quickly.[197]

'Political correctness is a catch-all term people apply to people who ask for more sensitivity to a particular cause than some are willing to give – a way to dismiss issues as frivolous in order to justify ignoring them.'[198]

'Where does white racial framing come from?'

Many find the origin of Hitchens' and others' idea of a 'liberal elite' in Spiro Agnew's (vice president under Richard Nixon) use of the phrase 'nattering nabobs of negativism'. Agnew was a US Republican, so to the right of the British Conservative party.

The Republicans, who generally were rich, having made their money by exploiting the working class, pointed out that Republicans and the working class were being oppressed by the 'liberal elite' of Democrats on the west and east coasts of US.

Republicans characterised the US white working class, and Republicans themselves by implication, as humble, reverent, courteous, cheerful, loyal, and regular workers. Republicans characterised their Democrat oppressors as parasites, representatives of the big business of Wall Street, arrogant and consumers of foreign ideas and food.

When the traditional working-class people of the Mid-West wanted to get their own back on big business, the Republicans encouraged them to believe that the Democrats were the problem, and therefore that they should direct their backlash against Democrats.[199]

Peter Hitchens often speaks at great length on TV programmes such as Question Time. One suggested response to his points is to say, 'No, Peter, we cannot return to 1914 just by the act of wishing really hard.'[200]

To those suffering pain because they see jobs and opportunities leaving their communities and staying away, many say that it is not primarily immigrants who are to blame. Rather it is the policies of successive governments on, e.g., privatisation, employment, regional inequalities, affordable and social housing, investment, austerity, military conflicts and trade unions. And companies' pay inequality and avoidance or evasion of paying taxes. These policies need to be challenged and changed for the better of everyone.

Chapter Eight. 'How did whiteness develop into Brexit?'

'Have you personally experienced more racism since Brexit?'

'Every day, mate. Yes, of course! Wolves come in sheep's clothing. You deal with it. You have to or you go mad. So long as you put one foot in front of the other, you're good' (emphasis mine) (Steve McQueen, British film director, 2018).[201]

'When I was in lockdown more and more the pieces started to fit together.... I'm one of the only ones that are around these people. So then I realised, it's not because you're annoying, it's not because you're ugly... it's because you don't look like them' (Natanya Popoola, 2020).[202]

People can view the white racial frame in Britain as a present-day expression of modernity. Modernity is a period from the mid-16th century in Europe. It is characterised by a rejection of tradition. By the prioritising of individualism. By a belief in scientific and technological progress. By a movement from feudalism into capitalism and hence to industrialisation and secularisation. And by the development of the nation-state.

It is also characterised by belief on the part of many people in various meta-narratives, for example capitalism, secularism and Marxism.[203] Looking at the white racial frame in Britain, people can see that frame as an expression of the culture of modernity that British people have grown up with.

The theme of the main white racial frame varies between countries. In US the main theme is the US nation, whereas in Britain the main theme is the British Empire, at its largest extent nearly one-quarter of the world's land.[204] Garner identifies four overlapping frames from people who responded to researchers' questions about how they viewed Britishness and immigration. Research took place in six provincial urban areas of England (Bristol, Plymouth, Birmingham, Runcorn/Widnes, Thetford and Milton Keynes).

Since 2000, research has shown that British people have become increasingly hostile to immigration. A range of people are viewed as immigrants, e.g., non-EU migrants (EU migrants are no longer categorised as immigrants in official statistics), asylum seekers and economic migrants. All people of colour are viewed as immigrants, even though many of them were born here and are not immigrants. Many people tend to roll all of these categories of immigrants together in their thinking about immigration.[205] People's views here are very often influenced by the tabloid press.

Frames provide three basic functions. Frames enable people to focus their attention through deciding what is relevant and what is irrelevant. Frames link elements of a story: people can edit a story, so that one set of meanings is communicated, rather than another. Finally, frames can transform ways in which people understand a situation, by re-ordering the story to convey a message different from what they had previously received.

Unfairness

David Cameron's Coalition government, which early on called for fairness, seemed only to administer unfairness. Many white people are saying that a situation is unfair when people get what they are not entitled to get, and those who are entitled to get this are prevented from getting it. 'Brits born in Britain' are being squeezed out, but people do not admit who is doing the squeezing, either because they do not know, or because they don't want to be seen as being racist.

One resource many people are looking for is housing. Two million of the 5.2 million social housing units were sold between 1981 and 2005, of which a million were sold by 1987, resulting in a house price boom. The 1981 Housing Act's prohibition on councils spending the money from house sales on constructing further social housing resulted in a social housing shortage.

The policy allowed property speculators to buy housing and sell it at a profit.

This shortage of social housing resulted in more people living in poor-quality private rented accommodation paid for through benefits, or with their family in overcrowded conditions. Because of the rise in house prices, people could no longer afford private housing. As a result, the rules for allocating the reducing stock of social housing were changed to a needs-based approach[206], rather than one based on a person's links to the local area in terms of their family or where they had previously lived.

By 2012, fewer than 1.7 million social housing units were available across England.[207] Most councils are operating a points system whereby people who are disadvantaged get more points. This has led to many white people feeling that people of colour, such as immigrants, are being preferred to them in getting social housing. Waiting lists had increased to 1.85 million households in 2012. However, the realities of social housing allocation are different from what many people think.

Applicants already in accommodation end up with better properties than those who need emergency accommodation, who are homeless or who are in overcrowded accommodation, and of whom many are people of colour and migrants.[208] In other words, white British residents seem to be advantaged. Further, the housing market can be hard to negotiate for those new to Britain so that relatively few migrants take up new lettings made available by social landlords.[209] So again, white, British applicants are advantaged.

The problems have been caused by the sales of council houses since 1981. This resulted in a private house building boom pushing up prices. Fewer people could afford to buy at these higher prices but no further social housing was being built. To avoid people blaming government policy, and in view of some people's concern about rising immigration, migrants were blamed for taking housing ahead of white British residents. Migrants were confused with people of colour, so racialising the discussion on housing. The right response would have been for government to build more social housing.

Another resource people try to get is a job. One argument made is that cheap migrant labour reduces other people's wages. However, figures that are available do not show who benefits and who loses out in the creation and loss of jobs.[210] Further, migrants put more into the economy in terms of taxation and what they spend than the benefits they take out.[211] Also, undocumented workers bring flexibility to the economy which helps it grow capacity.[212]

Concerning other resources, the message from the Coalition government from 2010 was that 'the money has run out'. It said that as a result, cuts in services and benefits were necessary to make up for what they considered was the over-bloated spending of the Labour government. The claim to be balancing the books was in fact cover for launching an attack on the working class and the poor.[213]

The Conservatives shifted the source of the problems in 2008 from the financial private sector to the public sector and from the structural risk-taking of investment banks to the excessive use of welfare by benefit recipients. The Conservative solution was radical cuts in the benefit system.[214] In this type of context people become sensitive to issues such as potential benefit manipulation, which can be blamed on immigrants.

The logic of entitlement underlies these claims of unfairness. Who gets resources and who deserves to get resources? This is based on thinking about the 'deserving' and the 'undeserving' poor, which goes back to mediaeval times. At that time, people who received public assistance did so on the basis of their physical condition and their commitment to hard work. People who were ill or too young or too old to work were looked after. Those finding it hard to get work were supported temporarily until they could get work.

Those deemed to be lazy or vagrants were not supported but punished instead. In modern Britain, whether you are deserving of receiving resources depends on whether you contribute or don't contribute. If you don't contribute, is it because you can't or that you won't?[215]

Some people are seen as being the 'idle poor'. The view is that people who are poor and are 'hard-working' get nothing from the system, while people who mess up their lives and others' lives get everything from the system, especially people living near the interviewee, such as kids at risk of going to prison or people on drugs but who don't work and get benefits, while the interviewee has to work. Interviewees often blame people who are not white for 'not contributing'.

This leads on to many white people's views on migrants. Migrants are seen as acceptable as long as they are seen to 'contribute', but as unacceptable if they do not 'contribute'.

Central to discussions on unfairness is the state, as distributor, patriarch and adjudicator. Could there be frustration at the fact that social housing is today a stigmatised and rare asset, whereas before 1981 social housing represented the working class being rewarded for its responsibility? The very slow recovery from the great recession of 2008 has been characterised by a low-wage economy and the working poor.[216]

Taking on very poorly paid work can be considered not worth it when losing one benefit under austerity can lead to losing others.[217] Interviewees see fairness as putting white British born in Britain at the front of the queue for resources. Notice that it is other working-class people of colour who come in for criticism, while the white middle class and white upper class, who have gained most from wealth redistribution in the last 30 years, escape all criticism.

Political correctness (PC)

For this point I will follow Malik as she shows how PC is crucial for understanding Britain after Brexit. In the 1980s a series of progressive reforms, such as treating people of colour, gay people and women with respect were made. These were attempts to deal with inequalities within British society. These reforms became known as 'political correctness' (PC) by the British ruling class, a way of speaking to people in a way that was more politically acceptable.

The 1990s saw a conservative backlash by that ruling class, stirring the working class into opposing these reforms. Sadly, today, as a result of this conservative backlash, the use of the term 'political correctness' has been changed to mean anything people want, as long as it means something negative. I will explain how PC works today.

First, the PC myth creates a grievance culture. In the UK the main fault line between people occurs on immigration. In the late 1970s Margaret Thatcher warned of Britain being 'swamped by people of a different culture'.[218] Immigration became seen as a threat to people's livelihoods. British politicians warned people that high immigration, Islamic extremism, less available social welfare and NHS failures resulted from PC and its evils. All these evils then got blamed on the EU which became a scapegoat for these grievances. The Brexit referendum was posed as a question on which culture British people wanted to live in.

Second, the PC myth had a fabrication arm in Britain's media. Making people jealous or angry sells newspapers. Parts of a story are often inflated into larger fake stories. PC myths are spread through stories, for example, about immigrants or gay people getting benefits.

A third element of the PC myth is the use of a tool known as Frequency Scrambling. It acts to divert people from looking at a true grievance to thinking about a false one. For example, there has been much discussion about the unacceptability of halal slaughter as being cruel to animals. However, the true issue is cruelty to animals prior to consumption.

Another example of a true grievance is that university syllabuses are ethnocentric, not fully inclusive and out of date. This has been turned into the false grievance of syllabuses being changed to include more people of colour writers. So, when, for example, people are asked to change the way they speak to women in the place of work, they end up talking about the men in the workplace who will be surprised about this and who will be feeling victimised.

Then there is a get-out card for people who are intolerant but who don't want to feel bad about it. They feel that they are not bigoted but rather that they have been unfairly stigmatised. But seeing one group as inferior to another is in reality part of traditional prejudice.

In a multicultural world, the progressive reforms of PC are the pains of growth as society works to provide for all of its members.[219]

Going back via Britishness and Englishness to the British Empire

Garner says Tony Blair and Gordon Brown gave speeches on Britishness apparently to try to recruit mainly British Asians to support British values in the wake of 9/11 and 7/7. David Cameron appeared to join their calls through speeches critiquing multiculturalism.

The British Empire resurfaced through the 200th anniversary of the abolition of the slave trade in 2007 and Blair and Brown's programme on Britishness. Interviewees have said that the Empire and its legacies are done and dusted. That some people did bad things to other people centuries ago that they shouldn't have done, but people shouldn't keep apologising for them. And it doesn't matter now anyway.

Britishness is seen as problematic by a majority of interviewees because it doesn't include a space for Englishness to be recognised. Gilroy sees Britain as being paralysed by looking back with melancholy to a past that has gone. This means looking back to a time before present-day diversity.[220] Britishness is congested with emotional debris, coming mainly from the legacies of empire.

Positive aspects of Britishness are seen to be areas such as determination, competitiveness, diplomacy and generosity. However, focusing on the armed services is a way to focus on white Englishness, which is strange considering the presence of troops from the Empire and Commonwealth fighting alongside British troops in 20th-century conflicts and up to the present day.[221] Britishness is a space abandoned to people seen as non-British. Meanwhile, Englishness is what people retreat to as a defence against invaders and weak government.

Many white British people feel under pressure to make apologies for what Britain did to many people during the Empire. However, those British people see making apologies as part of 'political correctness gone mad'. This 'no more apologising' approach sees empire as finished.

In the 2011 Census, people most identifying with Englishness rather than Britishness are no-religion White British people in the ethnicity table, and English Christians and Jews in the religious-affiliation table. Meanwhile those identifying more with Britishness than Englishness were Asian, Black or 'Other' in the former table and Hindu, Muslim and Sikh in the latter table.[222]

(Im)possible integration

The fourth frame focuses on (im)possible integration. Integration did not feature as part of government policy until the New Labour white paper, *Secure Borders, Safe Haven* in 2002.[223] There has been a national refugee integration policy since 2004, although refugees are only a small part of total immigrants. Castles et al. advised the Home Office that the main meaning of integration was a one-way adaptation of immigrants to the local culture.[224]

However, this contradicted the EU's Common Basic Principle 1 of immigrant integration in the EU, that integration should involve a two-way adjustment to each other by both immigrants and local residents.[225] Interviewees felt generally that they were making adjustments but that they couldn't see immigrants and non-white people making adjustments, so for white interviewees this appeared to be a one-way street with adjustments only made by local residents, so not what the British government was trying to achieve.

Interviewees generally favoured assimilation by darker people to a two-way adjustment. However, this was forgetting colonial encounters in which white people had tremendous power over colonial subjects[226] and ignored the tremendous advantage of holding an EU passport until Brexit.[227] There were frequent complaints that white people born in Britain were being moved out of symbolic rather than physical space, for example in Easton, Bristol, while the space became populated with darker-skinned people with dangerous ideas.

However, Easton today is still 60 per cent majority-white people.[228] Many white people then tend to use the Saudi Arabian regime as a stereotype to represent all Muslims in order to indicate the sort of intolerant approach towards difference that they believe English people should have towards immigrants to Britain.

Interviewees seem unconcerned that British people migrated en masse to and imposed their culture on and exploited colonies, yet, somehow, they feel that British tourists abroad today are not involved in any invasion. British migrants and tourists abroad are not seen as having any structurally embedded advantages as compared with migrants from the world to Britain.

How can people 'bond' effectively? If you're an English-speaking Christian you might have advantages compared with a Muslim, yet black Christian attempts to integrate into church congregations in Britain have been characterised by racist rejection.[229]

The integrator's invisibility involves their appearance and their absence of making public claims for difference. Appealing for receiving better treatment based on inequalities you experience is rejected by the logic of 'unfairness' above. Further, if white citizens perceive you as an asylum seeker or immigrant you have lost this ideal invisibility and are less likely to be able to integrate successfully.

Roy Jenkins, as Home Secretary, said in 1966, 'I define integration, therefore, not a flattening process of assimilation but as equal opportunity, accompanied by cultural diversity, in an atmosphere of mutual tolerance.'[230] Yet today, 'equality' has seemed to be replaced by 'unfairness'. 'Cultural diversity' is often seen as threatening rather than something of interest. With respect to 'mutual tolerance', it seems that the majority of interviewees' feelings are those of anxiety and resentment.

The majority of British white people seem to understand 'integration' as meaning 'assimilation', which sounds rather like cultural respect for people of other cultures equates to disrespect for British culture. This seems to be because Britain seems to have been conceived as a place where the first residents have the right to repel unwanted foreigners from its shore.[231] This is the opposite of how white people viewed the territories they colonised. This view decides who belongs, and who gets to say who belongs.

Further, while the phrase 'when in Rome, do as Rome does' is used by white people complaining about immigrants not integrating, this phrase is demonstrated to not apply to British people, whether historically or today, whether in Britain or abroad.

Summary of the four white racial frames in Britain

People have found in Britain (as in the US) that there is a discussion at the 'ordinary people' level about a white group whose hospitality is taken for granted, whose culture is not respected and for whom the things they are entitled to are being taken away by the elite and redistributed to minorities who are undeserving. This social discussion can be used as a political tool usually by mainstream parties, although in some countries also by parties of the far right for accomplishing their agendas.

Garner concludes that what makes political whiteness today is the state interacting in a relational process with the media and with both formal and informal political agents.[232] 'Social insecurity' has resulted from the degradation of full-time, permanent employment in the West.[233]

The involvement of people in welfare systems that they are increasingly likely to be dependent upon has increased their identification with the state[234] rather than with their political class.[235] So Western majority-white nations show their unionised workers that their interests are best served as part of the white nation's superior race, rather than by their identification with workers across 'race' and nations. Large-scale migration from the former colonies is faced by a nationalism that tries to keep resources for the indigenous white population.

It is crazy for people to think that white people are treated as if they were invisible, when white people are the majority of every parliamentary constituency! It is interesting that people think they are not being listened to because they are white, when a more plausible explanation might be because they are not near the top of the socio-economic ladder.

These four racial frames are a white counter-narrative to people of colour's traditional concerns about racism. Mainstream parties in government are responsible through their action for the pain people are feeling:

'neoliberal policies (i.e., dismantling the welfare state; promoting capital flight; privatising... schools, hospitals, housing, transit and other public resources; investing in police and prisons) are a form of state violence that produces scarcity, environmental and health hazards, poverty, and alternative (illegal) economies rooted in violence and subjugation.'[236]

Conclusions on whiteness in Britain

Some people have suggested that white British people have nostalgia for the Empire they have lost, which they see as the work of a civilising, entrepreneurial, economic leader of global trade. They forget the dark side of modernity, which is that colonialism, violence and genocide were directed towards people whose descendants have more recently come to this country.[237]

I would like to go beyond this to an analysis that says that whiteness is a psychosis to deal with the difference between the history of empire and values that white British people have been told that they had ('white mythologies'), and the actual reality of Western capitalism being set up and still operating today based on racial exploitation.

Psychosis is a disorder characterised by delusions and hallucinations. These delusions are 'false beliefs that the patient maintains in the face of overwhelming contradictory evidence'. This psychosis is characterised by irrationality so is not open to rational argument. The psychosis explains why, for example, many of the American founding fathers could declare liberty for everyone, while themselves owning enslaved Africans.[238]

Transition

Chapter Nine. 'Everyone's Eurocentric, aren't they?'

How did white people arrive at this point in their thinking and whiteness?

Many people believe in Eurocentrism, a belief that certain events had world-changing consequences. And that these events developed from within the culture and boundaries of Europe.[239] They see all other peoples and cultures as marginal or irrelevant.[240]

The separation between 'the West – led today by the US – and the Rest' rests on a history that misleads people into thinking that the West has unique characteristics. These characteristics are believed to show that the West is different from other countries and by implication that the West is superior.

The West's characteristics were believed to have developed independently from non-Western countries and enabled the West to become civilised and to civilise non-Western countries. These characteristics of the West that are thought to be uniquely Western include democracy, freedom, rule of law, tolerance, equality, human rights, rationality and humanism.

These characteristics are believed to have emerged through Greek and Roman empires, Christianity, the Renaissance and Enlightenment, the scientific revolution, the French revolution, the Industrial Revolution and modern democratic movements. This uniqueness to the West means that these characteristics are believed to have universal relevance. Any non-Western nation is therefore only ever seen as belatedly catching up with the West and frowned upon if seen in some way to be deviant in its application of European models.[241]

Connected histories

What people have discovered as they have studied further is that people shouldn't be thinking about there being a separation between ‘the West and the Rest’ with respect to these characteristics. Instead, that there have been interconnections and there are ‘connected histories’ between ‘the West and the Rest’ in the development of these values.[242]

For example, a major ‘discovery’ supposedly made by Europeans during the Renaissance was books written by Greek and Roman authors. However, these were actually mediaeval copies of books that had been used for centuries by Islamic scholars, who contributed much towards European understanding of the humanities and of humanism. European understanding is said to have been revolutionised by the printing press. Yet the printing press was invented in China and was later carried to Europe by Arabs.[243]

With respect to Renaissance art, artwork was traded in a worldwide market that developed from the 13th century, with art being traded both for inspiration and as a commodity. By researching how luxury goods circulated during the Renaissance, people see that places such as China, Japan, India, Persia and Istanbul were connected through commercial and political interests with Europe.[244]

With respect to science, there was a strong interchange of ideas between Muslims, Indians and Europeans in terms of cosmological and astrological ideas. This was repeated between 1400 and 1700 through the interchange of Latin and vernacular manuscripts relating to chemical and astronomic issues. For example, Copernicus is known to have consulted works by Islamic scholars such as Nasir al-Din at-Tusi and Ibn ash Shatir.[245]

Christianity has been seen as an aspect of unity for Europe. However, there has been a significant presence of Jews across Europe. There has been a significant presence of Muslims in Spain, Italy, the Balkans and Turkey for hundreds of years as a right of legitimate conquest. Turkey has been used as a mirror by Muslims to reflect back to them what Europe is like.[246]

With respect to the French Revolution, Europeans look back to this period as the source of the administrative structure of the nation state fanning out across Europe and from there, potentially, across the world.

However, before arriving at that time, people find that the decision to abolish slavery in the French Declaration of Human Rights in 1794 was triggered by a visit to France by a delegation from Saint Domingue which made the argument to the Constituent Assembly. This is also an example of the 'insurgent empire' working to bring change to the European 'mother country'. Sadly, slavery was reinstated in 1802 under Napoleon in French colonies.[247]

The assertion of national identity in the non-European world through becoming a nation state is historically joined to colonialism.

However, people also find that oppressive social policies are, as if in a laboratory, tested in the colonies before the coloniser imposes them in the European home country. For example, surveillance, report writing, intelligence gathering and fingerprinting were used in India, although surveillance had earlier been used by the Moghul emperor Akhtar. English literature was taught in India before it was taught in Britain, while general children's education was also instituted in India before being instituted in Britain.[248]

With respect to the Industrial Revolution, Britain was the first country to undergo an industrial revolution. The key element that demonstrated that the British Industrial Revolution was occurring was the financial results from the growth in exports of finished cotton goods. However, India had been the centre of world cotton production since 3000 BCE. The production of finished cotton goods became a focus through which Britain, as the leading imperial power in India, worked to deindustrialise India.

Several European countries set up east India companies from 1600 to take over and export production control of Indian cotton products. The British introduced a taxation system that penalised weavers who supplied any company other than the British East India Company. Under cover of protective tariffs European countries were able to copy and set up their own cotton weaving industries. In 1774 Britain passed a law saying that cotton cloth for sale in Britain had to have been spun and weaved in Britain.[249]

Technical innovations in spinning and weaving transformed the supply of finished cotton goods. Kay's flying shuttle doubled each weaver's output. Three innovations in spinning – Hargreaves' jenny, Arkwright's water frame, Crompton's mule and eventually

Roberts' automatic mule – meant advances needed to come on the weaving side.

Crucially steam engines were introduced for spinning and weaving. Bleaching started to be done using bleaching powder. Further, printing and dying were mechanised. Machine-made textiles from Britain and their rapid growth were to contribute to the deindustrialisation of India, whose textile industry was still based on labour-intensive methods.

Finished, British-manufactured textile products then fed into the transatlantic trade system having been produced from raw cotton grown in the American South through the labour of enslaved Africans. This reasoning is supported by a general equilibrium model that joins together manufacturing in Britain with land in America and enslaved Africans. American land was available in elastic (freely available) supply, while African labour was also an elastic resource. So raw material prices were driven up far less than if the raw material production had been in a closed economy.[250]

Shared values

With respect to values. Starting with democracy, ancient Mesopotamia had city states similar to those subsequently in Greece. India and China had similar forms of government, the latter more a being free, like a Robin Hood type. So also had tribes in Northern Ghana, such as the LoDagaa, and desert tribes in North Africa that relished freedom from chieftainship and central territory control. Democracy was also practised in Carthage and in Phoenician Tyre in the 2nd century BCE.[251]

Greek ideas of freedom are found in a range of Asian forms, such as protection for Brahmins in India and for Mandarins in China. Buddhism is egalitarian in its cultural aspects. Across Africa there was awareness of which people are subordinates and which have greater autonomy. An Englishman, Sir Adolphus Slade, serving in the Ottoman navy in the 1820s, compared a low-born person's freedom in the Ottoman Empire to rise to the level of pasha, to what was achieved in the French Revolution.[252]

With respect to the rule of law, this was quite common in oral cultures. Examples include in Australia, South Sudan, Botswana, the LoDagaa of Northern Ghana, and the Barotse (Lozi) of Zambia. Written cultures had their own methods, for example, registration and deeds. These methods were found in all societies after the Bronze Age. Written contracts have been used in China for, among other purposes, transferring land since the Tang period of the seventh to 10th centuries CE.[253]

Tolerance is the practice of plurality of religious belief. Ashoka, an Indian emperor, advocated tolerance as early as the third century BCE. One of a number of Islamic advocates of tolerance was Akhbar, the 16th-century Moghul emperor. He advocated human rights including, for example, freedom of worship. He also spoke against forced conversions. The millet system during the Ottoman Empire allowed religious communities to operate within their own jurisdictions. Muslims, Christians and Jews lived together in harmony in Islamic Spain during the mediaeval period.

In China, before the European Enlightenment, there was no dominant religion. Confucianism followed a secular approach. It provided an alternative to Buddhism or ancestor worship. Science did not come into conflict with religious beliefs.[254]

Equality, together with freedom and love, are basic features of Islam's ethical teaching. People have open access to opportunities. There is no religious group or priesthood that has advantaged access to truth. Further, even in the caste societies of India those who have fallen from twice-born status may be restored to a higher condition through bhakti (devotion).[255]

The international human rights agenda has primarily been pushed by countries among 'The Rest' against the opposition of 'The West'. Japan tried to introduce a human equality clause into the League of Nations' covenant in 1919. This was rejected by Western nations because their empires were based on the inferiority of their subject peoples. The Universal Declaration on Human Rights of 1948 was adopted by the United Nations General Assembly. However, the period since then has seen a considerable range of struggles for rights, particularly in Western democracies.[256]

Rationality is the ability to reason and apply logic. One element of Greek rationality was the syllogism, a form of sequential reasoning that is connected with inferring and proof in the following format, for example, All virtue is praiseworthy. Kindness is a virtue. Therefore, kindness is praiseworthy.

The challenge is that thinking in this form requires writing in a literate culture and for the speakers to have attended a school. It is difficult for a syllogism to be used in practice in an oral culture.

In developing an early form of syllogism, Mesopotamia preceded the Greeks in developing rationality by 1500 years. The first Indian example dates from around 250 BCE, slightly after the Greeks.[257]

Finally, humanistic scepticism towards religion is seen from the sixth century BCE in India. At that time there were atheistic groupings while agnostic Buddhism began and spread throughout East Asia. The *Ramayana* and *Upanishads* include sceptical views on religion.

Conclusions on Eurocentrism

Eurocentrism downplays expertise and skills passed on by people of Asia, Africa, Latin America and the Pacific Islands over many years. That wealth coming from the colonies helped finance industrial take-off. The massive contribution of enslaved and bonded labourers. And the way in which Africa, Asia and Latin America were deindustrialised and underdeveloped by European nations so that Europe could emerge supreme.

We've seen that the Eurocentric approach towards the history, achievements and values of white people fails to reflect the facts of what actually happened, since people of colour were involved in all of this. These traditional British histories, achievements and values are therefore an illusion. Some have called these histories, achievements and values 'white mythologies.'[258]

To understand history more clearly people need to recognise the contribution of non-Europeans – people of colour – to history by way of 'connected histories'. People also need to recognise the contribution of colonialism since the actions of colonised peoples actually changed policies in the mother country. That people of colour's history is British history ('we are here because you were there') in a way similar to how St. Domingue/Haiti's history needs to be recognised as part of French history.[259]

PART 3.

SOME ISSUES IN SCHOOLS

Chapter Ten. 'Underachievement' or Education Debt?

Ethnic inequalities in education – an overview (in addition to those in Chapter 3)

In state education in all countries of the UK the pupil population is more diverse than the population as a whole, owing to people of colour having a younger age profile than white British people. In 2020/21, across all schools, 27.7 per cent of pupils were people of colour. The rate of increase in pupils of colour is 1 per cent per year. In 20 or so years, therefore, pupils of colour could be the majority in schools.[260]

The 2019/20, GCSE grade figures for England showed a significant difference in attainment between different ethnic groups. Attainment 8 measures pupils' performance in eight GCSEs. The average score was 50.2 points out of 90 points. Chinese (67.6) and Indians (60.7) gained the highest scores. White British scored 49.7 points. Mixed white/black Caribbean (44.8), black Caribbean (44.0), Irish Traveller (31.8) and Gypsy/Roma (23.3) had the lowest scores.[261]

Many have criticised Prevent policies that target radicalisation as racialised surveillance of Muslims and South Asian pupils.[262]

Data from 2018/19 showed that white British students continued to be over-represented in apprenticeship starts, while all other ethnic groups continued to be under-represented.[263]

Students of colour disproportionately enter higher education (HE). They were 27 per cent of all university undergraduates in 2019/20.[264]

However, in 2019/20, while 85.9 per cent of white students achieved a 'good' degree (1st or 2 i), only 65.8 per cent of black students did so, an attainment gap of 20.1 per cent.[265]

With respect to staff working in HE, in 2017/18, all people of colour ethnic groups were under-represented.[266]

Achieving a UK Race Equality Mark (REM) is a possible way for HE institutions to improve race equality for staff and students of colour. However, achieving the REM is not compulsory, nor is it linked to other measures of teaching or academic excellence. So, the REM seems unlikely to be as successful in driving race equality as the Athena Swan Award has been in driving gender equality.[267]

Government and teacher responses to 'underachievement'

Thirty-five years after the Swann report, ethnic inequalities in schools are as persistent as ever. There is entrenched racial stereotyping, structural racism, low teacher expectations together with stereotyping, low educational attainment, ethnocentric curricula, and high levels of exclusions for some ethnic groups.[268]

At the heart of these inequalities has been the so-called 'underachievement' of black Caribbean children, and more recently Pakistanis.[269] The 'underachievement' of black Caribbean children has dominated government policy since the late 1960s.[270] Much research has been done into 'underachievement' of black Caribbean children.[271]

Much has also been written about the low expectations of teachers about the abilities of black Caribbean children.[272] This has not been helped by educational theories such as Bourdieu's about the 'cultural capital' of the middle class, which might suggest that black mainly working-class people might lack 'cultural capital', leading to deficit thinking.[273]

Instead, others, such as Maylor, Strand and Yosso have shown that black people have a different cultural capital, including aspirations for the future, linguistic skills, family and community history, networks of community resources, the ability to navigate through systems of inequality, resistance to racism and persistence in opposing oppression.[274]

As part of the development of race and of their whiteness, as in the Sir Keith Joseph example below, white people have created ways of hiding race by using other words.[275] So, people have developed ideas that denote the concepts of whiteness and blackness, where white is 'the Self' of the US and UK social frameworks and black is 'the Other'.

Conceptual categories such as 'school achievement', 'maleness', 'middle-classness', 'intelligence', 'beauty' and 'science' have become categories of whiteness, whereas conceptual categories such as 'gangs', 'basketball players', 'welfare recipients' and 'the underclass' have become the unacceptable categories of blackness. Blackness is socially constructed in opposition to whiteness,[276] so black people are once again positioned negatively compared with white people.[277]

To address this 'underachievement', government policy has mainly been to get black parents involved in supporting their child's learning, in terms of more aspiration, motivation, self-esteem and improved behaviour.[278] This is still blaming people of colour for their failure to achieve. Less attention, however, has been paid to educating teachers about black children's attainment and equipping teachers with the skills to deal with this 'underachievement', while showing how current school and teacher practices reinforce it.

The origins of 'underachievement' of black Caribbean pupils

In order to appreciate the argument, it is necessary to go back to the beginning of larger-scale immigration by people of colour to find the origins of their children's 'underachievement', recorded by Bernard Coard in 1971.[279]

Coard showed that the 'underachievement' of black children was due to the nature of the school system, rather than any failure on the children's part. First, overly excessive numbers of black children were being placed in 'educationally subnormal' schools (ESN). Pupils at ESN schools were considered unable to be academically successful. Expectations of them were low and their opportunities were limited. Black children were identified as ESN owing to culturally biased IQ tests and teachers' low expectations.

Teachers could seriously affect black children's performance in three main ways: by showing their prejudice, by being patronising and by having little expectation of their abilities. These attitudes were widespread. Being patronising, for example, could involve treating the black child like their pet, or saying, for example, that they were 'bright for a black child'. A teacher's low expectations and what they did as a result, such as putting black children in a lower teaching stream, got communicated to and internalised by those children.

The school curriculum focused on white, middle-class people only. The lack of any people of colour in the curriculum led black children to hate themselves and suffer psychologically. This was similar to the US situation, in which pre-school African-American children showed a preference for white dolls as opposed to black dolls.[280]

Having a lack of confidence that the British school system might improve, Coard recommended that black people should continue to operate supplementary schools to meet their children's needs. Although ESN schools have been closed, many of the other issues seem unchanged since 1971.[281]

'What has changed in education since Coard wrote in 1971?'

Around 1975 neoliberalism began in Britain, characterised by a sharp reduction in the public sector and its replacement by businesses run for profit.

Colour-blindness and focusing on white working-class underachievement

In 1985, Sir Keith Joseph rejected the recommendations of the Swann Report[282] (in turn a watered-down version of the Rampton Report[283] that the government had already rejected), refusing to take action specifically on inequalities in the education of pupils of colour. He assumed that all pupils' performance would inevitably rise as the performance of white British pupils generally was improved.[284]

In a similar focus on white British pupils, from time to time the media reports that low achievers in schools are white and British. The implication can be, 'Why are so many resources being given to pupils of colour when schools should be focusing on underachieving white working-class pupils?'

These media reports often fail to say that these low achievers are usually those receiving free school meals (FSM). FSM, which is a very crude proxy for poverty, is often not taken up by families of poor pupils of colour. The white FSM pupils are only historically about 14 per cent of white British pupils, and figures often include those for Irish Travellers and Gypsies. Their achievement is only marginally below those of black Caribbean pupils who have FSM. Further, the remaining 86 per cent of white British pupils do not receive FSM, and their academic achievement is ahead of virtually all other ethnic groups.[285]

Today, both the National Curriculum and Teachers' Standards support the government's colour-blind attitude in teaching.[286] Teacher education then requires teachers to adopt a colour-blind approach in order to enable classroom inclusion. However, colour-blindness results in teachers denying the significance of race in the lives of pupils of colour. This silences pupils of colour and results in teachers overlooking their contributions based on their experience of racism.[287]

Colour blindness is 'the system' forcing colour-blind policies onto teachers. It is therefore down to teachers to 'do it for the children' by recognising pupils of colour's experience of racism. Further, 42 British non-governmental organisations told the UN in 2016 that the government's colour-blind policies were increasing race inequalities in breach of the government's obligations under Article 1 of UN ICERD.[288]

In that it negates race[289], the curriculum that is colour-blind is 'potentially just as negative as a straightforward rejection of people with a different skin colour since both types of attitude seek to deny the validity of an important aspect of a person's identity.'[290]

Improvements

'This is all negative. What improvements have been made?'

Demie, McLean and Lewis's work showing which strategies have successfully improved the attainment of pupils of colour across a London inner city borough.[291]

The introduction of the REM (above).

Emdin's work on teaching methods (Chapter 12).

Many new black history materials for teachers (chapters 11 and 14).

Grime now mainstream in Britain.[292]

Explosion in buying anti-racist books, fuelled by protests against the death of George Floyd.

People of colour have led on each of these. They await the response of schools and the government.

Teacher education has changed

Through changes in teaching standards, teachers are no longer expected to make decisions based on their professional knowledge. Instead, they have become technicians focused on teaching their subject. Instead of university tutors being teacher educators, now they are teacher trainers. Much training is done through School Direct – through on-the-job school placements. If you study for a postgraduate degree you have to spend 24 weeks of the degree in school.[293] If the placement is in a predominantly white area the new teacher will be unlikely to develop race equality skills they could use subsequently in more ethnically diverse areas.[294]

References to race and ethnicity have disappeared from the Teachers' Standards. The creation of CATE (Council of the Accreditation of Teachers Education) led to the dropping of the conceptual framework underlying teacher education. The focus on teaching the subject has led to the silencing of discussion about, for example, race and gender equality. The emphasis now is on teaching your subject rather than helping teachers engage with a Britain that's becoming increasingly diverse.[295]

Many teachers are white and come from areas where their cultural and economic experience may not equip them to engage effectively with pupils of colour.[296] There is little attention given by initial teacher education (ITE) to diversity and black children.

Newly qualified teachers are known to feel inadequately prepared to teach pupils of colour.[297] It is also difficult to educate teachers in race equality at a time when teachers are discouraged from engaging with pupil difference and instructed to avoid undermining British values.[298]

Government policies little changed since 1971

Research in the US has shown that when white people are advantaged through systematic discrimination over many years, taking away those barriers to equality will not get rid of inequality, as inequality becomes locked in.[299]

Since the 1950s, successive British governments have refused to centre race equality in their education policy.

When we inspect the achievement of five or more A*–C grade GCSEs between 1989 and 2004 on a percentage point basis, we find that there is no improvement in black pupils' performance v. white pupils' performance. To improve, pupils would have to wait for 60 years, at which time white pupils would have already achieved 100 per cent.[300]

Of major importance is the continued use today of norm-referenced tests to assess pupils.[301] These rank pupils taking tests on a 'bell curve' – a normal distribution of scores that looks like a bell – a small proportion of pupils doing well, the majority performing average and a small proportion doing poorly.

To produce a bell curve every time, test questions are designed to emphasise the ways pupils perform differently from each other, not to find how they've learnt certain standards or material or acquired certain skills. Norm-referenced testing is made worse when people decide in advance what proportion of pupils will pass and what proportion will therefore fail the exam. So, my individual or school's success at passing comes at the expense of a less fortunate individual or a school's failure.

An alternative to norm-referenced tests are criterion-referenced tests. This tests performance against fixed standards or criteria. All pupils who achieve the pass mark against these criteria pass the exam. Examples include the ticks required for a car to pass an MOT test, or the standard needed for musical instrument grade exams. People need to lobby Parliament for the replacement of norm-referenced tests with criterion-referenced tests.

Teachers' and white pupils' views are little changed since 1971

In the UK, where white people form 86 per cent of the population according to the 2011 census, it is useful to look at the geographical spread of people of colour and at the ways in which people are separated.[302]

People of colour are largely located in *cities*. *Adjacent* areas are predominantly white areas within cities, where schools might be largely white. *Peripheral* areas are predominantly white areas next to cities, where white people, although using the city a lot, have less contact with people of colour. Most of the rest of the country is *isolated*, with few pupils of colour attending predominantly white schools.[303]

In the mid-1990s, first-year trainee student teachers were asked what they had heard said at school about people of colour. They gave examples of comments made, around 96 per cent of which were negative. The most common were, 'They should go back to where they came from'; 'If they come here, they should do things our way'; 'They're different and don't belong here'; and 'They smell.' People of colour were considered unwelcome since they were seen as troublemakers, and white people had difficulties with them owing to 'difference'. These stereotypes of British citizens of colour were by that time at least 40 years old.[304]

Researchers found that 10-year-old children admitted learning these comments from their older brothers and sisters or from teenagers slightly older than themselves. Gaine concluded that white pupils' views about pupils of colour would only change if schools changed them. Most school teachers were white. So, if white pupils did not change their attitudes towards people of colour in schools in predominantly white areas of the country, nothing would change as a result in cities.[305]

When white student teachers began their training, they did so very often with views about people of colour that they had picked up in secondary schools. Situations have not changed much since, in terms of white teachers coming from predominantly white areas. The 1990s saw a backlash from Conservative governments that reduced funding to university teacher training courses and local education authorities, leaving new teachers to learn from existing teachers' views on race while on school placements.[306]

The Race Relations Amendment Act (2000) followed the report of Sir William Macpherson and required schools to implement race equality policies and to monitor and report racist incidents. This duty was replaced by the Public Sector Equality Duty which followed the Equality Act 2010 and which required schools to publish their equality schemes on race. But owing to government policies, schools today have no requirement to address race equality. The establishment of new schools, such as free schools, faith schools and academies, has encouraged deregulation and a lack of monitoring as regards issues of equality.

Also, schools are required to promote 'fundamental British values', such as 'democracy, the rule of law, individual liberty and mutual respect and tolerance of those with different faiths and beliefs'.[307] Many have seen this as cultural imperialism and the imposition of white superiority over people of colour.[308]

Further, schools have been required, under the Prevent Duty, to report on any individuals vulnerable to radicalisation. This discriminates against Muslims and changes a school's responsibility from that of pastoral support to vigilant spying. Additionally, a course on citizenship must be taught, including both 'fundamental British values' and the Prevent agenda. These are all examples of whiteness, that sees white people as 'the Self' and people of colour as 'the Other', thereby reinforcing white supremacy.[309]

Considering the way in which the educational system has failed successive generations of pupils of colour, people should view this not so much as 'underachievement' by pupils of colour but as an education debt that successive governments owe towards pupils of colour, including black Caribbeans and Muslims.[310]

CHAPTER ELEVEN. TEACHERS AND RACIAL LITERACY

'To be a negro in this country and to be relatively conscious is to be in a state of rage... almost all of the time — and in one's work. And part of the rage is this[.] It isn't only what is happening to you. But it's what's happening all around you and all of the time in the face of the most extraordinary and criminal indifference... of most white people in this country, and their ignorance' (James Baldwin, 1961). [311]

Helping teachers on their journey in racial literacy

First, it would be helpful to increase the numbers of teachers of colour, meaning more new teachers of colour going through teacher training. Further, it is necessary to look at any racisms in both recruitment and hiring processes.

White teachers form 91.4 per cent of all teachers in England's state-funded schools[312] so should be involved in tackling racism in schools. Antiracism is the responsibility of teachers of all backgrounds. Teachers will need to have racial literacy. This means they will need to understand how race and racisms operate in society. They will also need to have the language and skills to use their knowledge in their teaching.

Seeing how racism operates in society involves looking beyond acts of prejudice to see structural racism woven into society's institutions. Understanding this, teachers can go on to see how the education system itself reproduces racist inequalities. Racial literacy involves people in a journey and should be part of continued professional development (CPD).

Racially literate teachers will need to go beyond colour-blind approaches. They will need to see anti-racism and doing away with institutional racism as being of prime importance. They will need to see the ways in which their own whiteness can work to reinforce racism in schools. They will look to rid themselves of stereotypes of pupils of colour and of low expectations of their attainment, and thereby to avoid putting them into lower sets for studies.

They will therefore avoid racialised expectations that lead them into making low assessments and moving them towards disciplining and expelling pupils. This move towards racial literacy should be part of a whole-school approach.[313]

In order to act to improve teachers' ability to work as effectively in the classroom with black Caribbean, Muslim, Travellers and Roma pupils as they are working with white British pupils, intervention needs to take place at different levels. One level is that of training teacher educators. Another level is that of training new and existing teachers. A further level is that of engaging with so-called underachieving groups in the classroom. This also has implications for the curriculum taught.

White people need to take responsibility for doing this work. People of colour risk losing far more, in terms of relationships, job, income, home and worse when someone complains about them for what they have said than white people.[314] Only 8.6 per cent of teachers in England are people of colour.[315]

How whiteness blocks the way to racial literacy

The organising concept that undergirds the policy, practice and curriculum of teacher education is whiteness. Whiteness is invisible to white people. Whiteness is a system of power gathered by white people through colonisation and globalisation. This domination of white people over people of colour has led to the perpetuation of advantage of white people over people of colour in the structures of society.[316]

Whiteness is 'an amalgamation of qualities including the cultures, histories, experiences, discourses and structurally embedded advantages shared by Whites.... no White person can escape its influence.'[317]

To see the effect of whiteness on ITE, Lander interviewed 25 teacher educators at a university in a predominantly white area of England. She asked them to comment from their experience on what were the bridges and barriers to race equality in ITE.[318]

Of the 25 teacher educators or tutors, most had forgotten any education about race equality they had received during their own personal experience of ITE. Further, 20 of the 25 had limited experience or no experience of teaching in multi-ethnic areas. This shows a common lack of knowledge about ethnicity, race and racism. The whiteness they reveal in their discussions can be analysed in terms of denial, deflection, colour blindness, protection of white domination, innocence, niceness and ignorance. This builds on Picower's research into teachers' views.[319]

Many tutors wanted to protect students from understanding race and racism. Tutors made excuses as to why race and racism didn't come up on the ITE curriculum or in student teachers' practice. Some tutors felt that white student teachers had a lot to do in learning how to become teachers without being burdened in terms of teaching race equality. Others said that student teachers were good people but were afraid of getting things wrong when teaching about racism.

One tutor said that student teachers attending their university were coming from another predominantly white area. One implication of what he was saying could be that being at a university in a predominantly white area, the student teacher shouldn't expect to learn about race equality. Other possible implications included why would they want to learn about race equality, especially if they expected in future to work in a predominantly white area?

Other tutors said existing teachers in schools were not sufficiently experienced in teaching race equality to be able to support student teachers in teaching race equality. Most ITE now takes place in schools under the management of School Direct[320] and under the supervision of existing school teachers. So, university ITE tutors might be absolving themselves of the responsibility of teaching student teachers how to teach race equality.

A number of tutors saw colour blindness as a respectable viewpoint. They talked about people as part of a 'common humanity' and saw ethnicity as only related to external characteristics, such as skin colour, which they saw as irrelevant to learning. They saw ethnicity as a hindrance, so a teacher's goal should be to make 'those pupils invisible'. However, colour blindness is a way to deny ethnic identity. By doing this it centres white identity as the norm, so white identity becomes the identity to preserve.[321]

Some tutors spoke about other tutors who saw the student teacher as a saviour who could save pupils of colour from obstacles such as racism and language.[322] One tutor spoke about the 'goodness of primary teachers' while discussing a Muslim student teacher failing on their placement.

Another tutor spoke of a racist incident on the course she was teaching as having been blown up out of proportion. Another tutor spoke of treating ethnicity as a label while she warned about the danger of using labels. Later in the discussion, however, she referred to herself by the label of 'white working class'. This shows how whiteness works to remain the dominant discourse.

One way whiteness operates is in respect to the retaining of student teachers of colour. Student teachers of colour have to navigate racism from existing teachers, pupils and schools in order to survive their placement and pass their course. They are struggling against institutional racism which whiteness in ITE acts to strengthen.[323]

Ways forward related to teacher educators and student teachers

Government reform of teacher education has made ITE more school based and subject teaching focused, in that, for example, student teachers often receive only a one-hour session on race. Lander sees this as an example of structural racism. Teachers are not being equipped to handle racist incidents nor with how to teach diversity in the curriculum. Racist bullying, some examples of which are shown in the Introduction, has been met with comments from teachers to pupils who are bullied such as, 'Just ignore it. Stay away from them.'[324]

The following approach is suggested for training both teacher educators and student teachers.

Traditional thinking and the context of cultural diversity

A common educational approach has been to treat pupils of colour as 'just like white pupils', but to recognise them as 'disadvantaged' and act as if they need compensatory and remedial education in order to achieve success. However, educators of colour say teachers need to see that the worldview that underlies their understanding of teaching is stopping them from communicating effectively with pupils who have a quite different worldview from that of their teachers. [325]

Cultural diversity training was popularised in the early 1970s. The belief is that teachers need fixing, rather than pupils.

'We are dealing... not so much with culturally deprived children as with culturally depriving schools. And the task to be accomplished is not to repair deficient children but to... transform the... operations of the schools to which we commit these children.... To continue to define the difficulty as inherent in the raw materials – the children – is plainly to blame the victim and to acquiesce in the continuation of educational inequity.'[326]

Cultural difference does not imply either deprivation or deviance. Multicultural education recognises that people in Britain, like America, are multicultural, not only by racial and cultural mix but by identification with common needs, interests and concerns. It is to this sense of identification that education must be developed. It must function within a changing social scene that is aware of and sensitive to cultural diversity, and, at the same time, it must realise that all cultures interact with and may have implicit commonalities with all others.[327]

Using a model to test student teachers' suitability to work with culturally diverse pupils

Goodwin suggests that teacher educators and student teachers should go through a six-phase model to identify whether they are willing to work sensitively with culturally diverse pupils.[328] The six phases are:

1. To look within at their personal history, to see what their cultural values and biases are.
2. To learn about multicultural teaching and cultural learning styles.
3. To study the interaction of race, gender, class, etc., within the economic system today. Critical studies include, for example, Helms.[329] This is a 'lighting fires under student teachers' phase.
4. To reflect and re-assess after phase 3 above. What were teachers thinking about educational equity before and after phase 3?
5. Thinking and acting differently. Teachers decide to learn anything so as to make a difference.
6. Return to phase 1. How does our new understanding change our story?

Phase 1 above might go on for several months. The bonding that results is needed when people are struggling through phase 3.

This model helps teachers past a multiculturalism that tinkers at the edges of change. Making this transition from myself to others begins not through knowing others but by knowing myself.

Looking from the standpoint and aspirations of long-term resident people of colour

Communities of colour in England and Wales numbered 7.9 million people in 2011, or 14 per cent of the population.[330]

These are people who have lived in Britain for 30 years or more. Further, these are mainly peoples with whom Britain has had a long-standing relationship going back some hundreds of years through colonialism. These people are predominantly part of British history or the history of another colonising country.[331]

When considering colonialism, today's neo-colonialism and structural racism in Britain, it is important to recognise the children from these families as being victimised and traumatised by both the society and educational system in Britain or another colonising country.[332]

To teach in a way that is relevant to these pupils in our multicultural society requires people to start by understanding their culture. To teach in a culture-centred way involves learning the history of people of colour's challenges to and transformation of British cultural practices that dehumanise people of colour.[333] So, social criticism is an important academic skill. In order for people of colour to achieve academic excellence, education must operate for the liberation of pupils of colour and for transforming society.[334]

Strategies and resources to support pupils of colour's achievement[335]

Use research findings from schools that have successfully raised the attainment of pupils of colour, for example,

- 'the importance of high-quality school leadership, a school ethos that embraces diversity and has high expectations of all pupils, monitoring and tracking of pupils, a flexible and inclusive curriculum, and engagement with parents and the wider community'.[336]

Also, give opportunities within the curriculum for pupils to see how their heritage has contributed to civilisation. Some examples of resources are:

Our Migration Story, how migrants shaped British history over 2000 years.

Bennie Kara (2020). *A little guide for teachers: diversity in schools*, how to create a diverse curriculum, across or within subjects.

The Historical Association – resources for teaching black history at KS 1, 2 and 3. The Royal Historical Society (2018).

Race, Ethnicity and Equality Report. Pupils of colour are less likely than white pupils to choose to study history for exams. This report helps to overcome this barrier.

The Black Curriculum has produced free resources for teaching black history, covering 12 topics and four modules for KS 2 and 3.[337]

The Indus Valley Civilisation lasted from 3300 BCE to 1300 BCE in north-west South Asia. It can be studied at KS 2.[338]

The 1947 Partition of India and Pakistan followed two centuries of British rule. It resulted in 14 million people being displaced and between one and two million being killed. The BBC has a section called 'Partition stories', including eye-witness accounts. *Newsround* has information on what happened and why. The National Archives has copies of original documents. The BBC has recordings of Nehru, Jinnah and Mountbatten. The British Pathe Historical Collection has archived films. Bangla Stories has stories of people in Bengal after independence. The Partition Education Group enables more engagement with the Partition. It is part of the South Asian Heritage Month initiative.[339]

1001 inventions is a website accompanying the book *1001 Inventions: The Enduring Legacy of Muslim Civilisation* (Al-Hassani, 2012). It covers how, during the Islamic Golden Age, the concept of zero came from India via China to the Middle East; how surgical tools were developed; how algebra was developed and how the first university was founded in Morocco.[340]

It is important to deal with racism, including bullying. Resources are available from NATRE, the Runnymede Trust, Show Racism the Red Card, EqualiTeach, EHRC, the Crown Prosecution Service and Kick It Out.[341]

Then, work towards achieving a race equality award as a school. This enables a school to audit and evaluate practice to ensure race equality is at the heart of what they do.

Again, be proactive in engaging with parents and the local community. Young people only spend 15 per cent of their time in school so the school must build bridges with parents. Key factors for success in engaging with parents are having a holistic approach, using dedicated resources, recruiting pupils and parents locally and building social capital.[342]

Further, develop strong relationships with supplementary schools in the neighbourhood. These might be for religious instruction, supporting language or providing curriculum support for pupils from these heritages and cultures.[343]

Also, if the school is not diverse, establish a School Linking relationship. This can develop awareness, respect and critical thinking skills.[344]

Finally, look at reading texts and ensure they show pupils of colour in a positive way rather than reinforcing stereotypes.[345]

CHAPTER TWELVE. METHODS OF TEACHING LEADING TO LIBERATION

Culturally Relevant Pedagogy (CRP), originated by Ladson-Billings[346], is a method of teaching that is all about opposition, that is, resistance to oppression, and is committed to collective, not just individual, empowerment. This method of teaching includes pupils' cultural backgrounds, experiences and interests in all forms of teaching and learning.

CRP rests on three characteristics: pupils must be achieving academic success; they must develop and maintain their cultural competence; and they must develop their critical consciousness so that they can challenge the status quo in society. Arshad gives examples of CRP being used in Glasgow in 2020.[347]

Emdin (2016) argues that the CRP approach, that of considering pupils' culture in deciding ways in which they should be taught, cannot be achieved unless teachers widen their scope way beyond traditional classroom teaching. The focus is on urban areas, where pupils of colour are more numerous, yet most teachers are white. The context is working to improve pupil achievement on the one hand, while preparing pupils to use science, technology, engineering and mathematics (STEM) skills in their future career, on the other.

The similarities of experiences and standpoints between different people of colour have helped develop a response to CRP. The response is Reality Pedagogy, that is, a reality method of teaching. This meets each pupil on their emotional and cultural turf. The pupil is the expert at their own learning and teaching, while the teacher is the learner. The pupil shapes how to best teach the content, while the teacher delivers the content. The teacher and pupil together construct and implement a plan for how that classroom will be used to deliver the teaching.

The approach is of West African origin and is modelled on the call and response in the black church between the preacher and congregation, leading to focus and engagement, and the altar call, which results in reflection. This Pentecostal approach shows how a teacher can share what they know so that people can receive it in the most effective way.[348]

This approach is paralleled by MCs in hip-hop who use call and response to draw in an audience. Both MCs and black preachers use music to engage the audience and share information. Workers in barber shops and beauty salons also use call and response to engage emotionally and be a teacher with valued clients.

The British equivalent musical context to US' hip-hop is Grime. Grime's origins are in Jamaican reggae deejays chanting or talking over an instrumental rhythm. Further back, they come from West African history and storytellers chanting over a drum beat.[349]

Seven tools of Reality Pedagogy (RP): seven C's

Cogenerative (cogen) dialogues

Cogenerative (cogen) dialogues use rap cyphers – a codified method of dialogue between people of colour – and culture circles to increase pupil involvement and performance.[350] The teacher meets with a group of four pupils, representing the range of diversity and achievement in the class, to plan with the pupils how they will all work together to deliver the work content so that it meets pupil requirements. After a few meetings, the teacher asks one pupil to invite another pupil to join the group, while asking that original group member to stand down and take up an important role in the classroom, e.g., operating a video recorder.

Co-teaching

Co-teaching has traditionally meant at least two teachers sharing the teaching of a classroom. However, this has failed to close the achievement gap or make pupils of colour feel the teacher is connecting with the way they are thinking. In RP the second teacher is a pupil. A chief goal is to help the teacher teach so as to reflect the needs of the pupil. The teacher learns to do this by being taught by the pupil. 'Is this teaching job so easy that a pupil can do it?' No. A postgraduate degree is necessary if you are to learn to teach. However, if you're a white teacher who's teaching pupils of colour, you need to learn much more.

A study of indigenous forms of communication by Hawaiian youth, including overlapping speech and rhythmic conversation indicated that using these forms of communication in the classroom supports pupil learning. Further, a study of African-American children showed that using the language and experiences of youths positively impacted teaching.[351] For youth experience and language to be best used, youths must do the teaching.

The teacher should let the pupils know that they have very valuable teaching skills. Two or more pupils are asked to take a lesson and to do all that the teacher does. They must write a lesson plan in line with standards, identify examples to be used, find teaching resources and find a method for assessing their teaching. To help with this, the teacher provides the co-teaching pupils with preceding lesson plans, teacher manuals, websites for resources and all other teacher materials. Co-teaching pupils are then graded based on their teaching methods.

The teacher invites two or more pupils to co-teach, probably in the cogenerative dialogue meeting, gives them a quick tutorial on the concept of the lesson and assigns them to write a lesson plan rather than the usual homework assignment. The next day the teacher reviews their lesson plan and invites them to teach the lesson.

The teacher sits in a seat normally occupied by a pupil and does not interrupt the lesson. If there is a point that the teacher needs to correct or clarify, the teacher should raise their hand and ask a question in a respectful way. Meanwhile the teacher should follow the lesson very carefully, noting the points at which the pupils do their teaching differently from the teacher, e.g., the examples used, and work out how to change their teaching methods to align with the pupils' methods.

Cosmopolitanism

Cosmopolitanism in the classroom starts with pupils feeling themselves connected to the universe and hence feeling valued and respected as full and active citizens of the classroom space they occupy. The teacher identifies roles that pupils can perform so that the class can function properly and meet its academic, emotional and social goals.

Roles might include arranging desks, sweeping floors, organising teaching materials and ensuring technology is working. Pupils are given academic credit for how they perform these roles. This is contrary to traditional teaching, which focuses solely on academic grades and individual achievement. However, pupils of colour recognise that they are supporting their fellow pupils and community and feel far more committed to doing well in class as a result.

Teachers in urban areas are primarily white, middle-class women. Only 8.6 per cent of all teachers in England are teachers of colour and three-quarters of all teachers are women.[352] Teachers of any background who feel vulnerable in the presence of pupils of colour are likely to exert power over pupils and become strict in their discipline. The current system traditionally rewards teachers and pupils who assimilate into a homogeneous pupil identity of 'sitting quietly on your own'. Pupils of colour who instead speak loudly with their friends are likely to be shamed, even if they're trying to help other pupils, with their answering a maths question, for example.

Teachers look favourably on pupils whose behaviour reminds them of themselves, but this is counter to how many pupils of colour are. The teacher has created an anti-cosmopolitan classroom. Further, by learning that being docile and passive is the right thing to do in the classroom, pupils of colour who comply with this can be conditioned towards assimilating into the white middle class and ultimately losing their self-worth.

While the teacher believes being quiet is 'smart behaviour', a pupil of colour who sees being loud as smart is likely to be penalised in terms of how the teacher grades them academically. Instead of separating pupils based on teachers' ideas of what is 'smart' behaviour, Emdin suggests moving towards a classroom where no pupil models the norm but every pupil shapes the norm. Pupils build a connection to one another and to the classroom that values where they stand racially, ethnically, academically and emotionally.

Traditionally the teacher fights throughout the year against ways of moving, talking and gesturing that bring pupils together but which the teacher sees as disruptive behaviour. However, at the end of the academic year, the teacher no longer has to teach to strict guidelines and as the classroom feels more cosmopolitan, pupils react differently and the teacher starts to engage pupils more effectively. By developing cosmopolitanism, the teacher can now enjoy the celebration and camaraderie that's currently only available at the end of the year, throughout the year. How can they do this?

First, teachers will need to use language that is rooted in the culture of people of colour, to reinforce the idea of a shared community, even though that language originates outside the classroom. This is likely to be achieved by using call and response, with an emphasis on overcoming challenges and pupils being strong when facing obstacles.

Call and response is key within the black church, hip-hop and Grime. So, one person saying, "Every day I'm" might receive the response, "hustling", when they were trying to shake off sleep and work harder to get tasks done.[353] Similarly, the call, "I will not lose", popularised by Jay-Z and other rappers, is answered with the repetition of, "I will not lose" to motivate people to overcome obstacles.

A second way of encouraging cosmopolitanism in the classroom is through what Emdin calls 'the cosmo duo'. This is based on two pupils working together, each supporting the other when they individually find classwork challenging.

When the four pupils in the cogen group have attended three sessions of the group, they will have developed a relationship with each other. The teacher then invites them to pair off with another member of this group in such a way that there will be one academically strong pupil and one academically weaker pupil in each cosmo group. These cosmo groups will continue alongside working together in the cogen dialogues.

The pupils in cosmo groups are then encouraged to share their strengths and weaknesses as regards the different elements of the classroom. If both pupils have the same strengths and weaknesses, the teacher encourages them to link with another pupil who is able to help them address the areas they need help with.

After a short while, the teacher gives these cosmo duos the opportunity to share with the whole class how they've improved by working together and what they have been able to do through working together outside of the school context. Then the teacher encourages pupils to reflect on their strengths and weaknesses and find someone who might be able to help and work together with them in a cosmo duo. The teacher works with each cosmo duo to facilitate their planning of how they will work together and on what.

The teacher lets pupils who are academically stronger know that their test scores will increase by the same amount as they increase the scores of the weaker cosmo duo member. So, while in traditional classrooms the teacher focuses on the success of individuals, cosmo duos instead enable all pupils to raise their performance while they achieve other communal goals, such as deepening cosmo duo partnerships.

Another practical tool for encouraging cosmopolitanism is for class pupils to be a replacement family that supports pupils' socioeconomic and academic aspirations. Very often children miss a strong family to provide this support. The concern here is that a replacement family, such as a gang, steps in and leads pupils astray.

Finally, cosmopolitanism can be shown through non-verbal communication. Examples include handshakes, head nods and how people look at each other. In traditional classrooms there is a focus on pupils raising their hand and waiting for approval to speak from the teacher. In a cosmopolitan classroom there is a more free-flowing interaction and sharing of cultural practices. Touch has been found to be associated with improving educational and relational outcomes.

Context and content

Researchers, such as Bourdieu, call these cultural practices social capital.[354] They say that people have social capital that results from their shared background and experiences. People then exchange social capital with each other for their communal benefit in different social fields.

So, if a teacher asks pupils to do something which is too difficult or in their opinion of no use, pupils of colour coming from the local area may well respond by eye-rolling and non-verbal communication with pupils from a similar background. However, the risk is that they may lose the opportunity to exchange capital with the teacher or the school.[355]

In the same way as pupils exchange social capital within their networks, schools and teachers share social capital within their own networks. The risk for educators and teachers is that they fail to connect to pupils' living contexts and networks.

Emdin's learning moment happened when after school had finished one day, he left lesson planning and classroom management behind and went outside to play basketball on a local court with pupils from the local area. Doing the same the next day, then being invited by them to neighbourhood events, helped him incorporate what he was learning from pupils' experiences of living in the area into his daily teaching, which revolutionised it.

He says there are three steps educators need to take to engage with pupils' contexts. The first is being in the same social space as pupils of colour. Educators should start by visiting businesses that pupils frequent. Then move to places further away from the school and nearer to pupils' communities, such as churches and community centres, and walking through the neighbourhoods, observing what is happening.

The second step is engaging with the pupils' context. This involves hard work. For example, asking pupils questions to check that what you think you've observed is right. Recognising non-verbal cues that pupils give each other, asking what the cues mean, practising them and anticipating when cues are coming.

The third step is to make connections between pupils of colour's contexts and the content you are supposed to be teaching. Making these connections helps to heal a break in the relationship pupils of colour have with schools and teaching.

This will involve, for example, bringing in artefacts that pupils are familiar with from their neighbourhood. These artefacts could be symbolic, such as phrases they say or gestures and cues they make, or descriptions of people or things that you can't bring from the neighbourhood to the classroom. Or the artefacts could be tangible – objects that can be brought in from the neighbourhood, e.g., rocks from a park or pictures of lifts in flats or graffiti.

Using these examples will ease pupils' understanding of STEM and other subjects. There will be a close correlation between the time educators spend engaging with their community and how long pupils of colour engage in the educator's class.

When pupils explore the relationships between their own context and the content of the lesson, they might ask a question that the teacher cannot answer. For example, they might ask what are the origins of geometry and who decided what shapes to use in building constructions and why. This can result in a classroom in which some teachers might view matters as getting out of control. Teachers should not worry about this. Here are three ways of dealing with this.

Teachers should welcome unusual ways of expressing content knowledge, for example by using slang or loudness. Further, teachers should allocate a space on a board where pupils can post questions that they would like an answer to, and those that a teacher could not answer. Finally, any pupil posting questions or answers to these questions should gain extra marks.

Competition

When people of colour in society have issues with other groups they encourage their youth to settle disagreements by showing how well they know their own culture. The response to these issues is one that is competitive, yet collaborative and peaceful. Grime has origins in the soundclash culture of Jamaica which involves competing sound systems facing off to see who the crowd consider the best.[356] Pupils of colour encounter what Bourdieu and Wacquant call symbolic violence in traditional classrooms.[357] This is a socio-emotional violence where your spirit is broken owing to constantly being held in a system that runs contrary to your worldview.

In the classroom the Grime battle can be used to let everyone learn by doing so actively through teaching and learning, thereby creating cultural learning experiences. This is a way of building and supporting the community to be successful together, rather than as in the traditional classroom, which is focused on who is the best individual. The focus is also on what the pupil can say on the subject matter, rather than on studying and writing, as in the traditional classroom.

The Grime battle can take place across schools. The purpose is to engage with pupils of colour who are often disengaged from science as it is traditionally taught, and give them the opportunity to use their passion for Grime in talking about science. This can be taken across schools. It involves a teacher going into classrooms and suspending the usual assessment method for a particular learning unit. Instead, pupils are asked to write a poem or chat about the science content they are learning, and are assessed on what they write. The educator can invite a local Grime artist to help to organise the battle.

Showing your brilliance in speaking rather than writing is a great strength of people of colour. For example, Thomas Fuller, an illiterate enslaved man, could not read or write but was able to outshine others by giving accurate verbal answers to mathematical questions. There is a history of community support for developing black mathematicians.[358]

Curation

Curators are managers charged with presenting a museum's collections and interpreting these collections for the public. Often collections have been taken by white people from the territory of people of colour. People of colour from the same or a nearby culture are far more understanding of these artefacts and of the culture, so it makes more sense for people of colour to curate such collections. Similarly, when pupils curate their own experiences of school they benefit, and so do teachers. The urban teacher's responsibility is to enable pupils of colour to curate their own experiences. These experiences then become tools to help both pupils and teachers teach.

A good way for pupils to curate their school experience was shown when one of the cogen group used video she had taken to show Emdin he was yelling at his pupils. This enabled him to reflect more and follow the cogen group's advice to cure himself of yelling.

Another way for pupils of colour to curate their experiences is through social media. Black Twitter, for example, is a good place to learn how pupils of colour experience and react to daily life, when they might not be so forthcoming in a classroom.

For educators who block social media from educational use, Emdin has experimented with paper forms of digital platforms. He is then able to conduct teaching in conjunction with pupils using paper forms of Twitter and Instagram. Using historical pictures in a contemporary language in Instagram format brings pupils of colour into the content being taught in powerful ways. It also provides the teacher with curated archives for future teaching.

Metalogues merge social media-type exchanges by pupils with artefacts that pupils curate, in such a way that pupils are more engaged and the teacher can better understand what is going on in the classroom. The structure is like the cogenerative dialogue, but takes place through written communication between pupils and the teacher.

The teacher buys notebooks for groups of four pupils that stay in the classroom throughout the year. The four pupils reflect the diversity of background and ability in the class. When the teacher asks for a metalogue, this might be about anything, such as the content being taught, a review of the lesson, how pupils feel things are going or similar.

The groups of four have pre-assigned colours of pens reflecting their diversity, and respond to the teacher's prompt question, separating what they write from each other by an ellipsis (three dots). The teacher can then at any time pick up a group notebook and assess individual pupils' learning and respond to these comments without having to wait for a test.[359]

CHAPTER THIRTEEN. POLICE IN SCHOOLS AND THE SCHOOL-TO-PRISON PIPELINE

Introduction

Concerns about 'knife crime' have led the Home Affairs Select Committee on Youth Violence to recommend a dedicated police officer be appointed at every school in areas of serious youth violence. The Children's Commissioner has subsequently asked for 'neighbourhood police officers [to be] attached to every school'.[360]

Some teachers have responded to this call for a police presence in schools. For many pupils, schools are places of sanctuary. A police presence would disrupt that sanctuary for over-policed communities of colour. Pupils of colour are disproportionately stopped and searched, even though researchers have shown this to be ineffective at preventing crime.[361]

Some teachers consider more police in schools to be more likely to criminalise pupils and produce delinquency than stop it. The stigma of police in schools is more likely to be experienced by working-class pupils and pupils of colour. Pupils of colour are already subject to racial discrimination at school as regards disciplining. It would seem that police presence might emphasise a move towards a schools-to-prison pipeline, as in the US.[362]

A police presence in schools may result from a concern about terror and Islam, as shown in the Prevent Duty, which produces 'racialised surveillance of Muslim and South Asian pupils'. This would probably cause concern on the part of South Asian and Muslim pupils.[363]

Some teachers feel that a police presence could be more positive if officers were in schools in a supportive, community-relations role. However, there is little evidence that this is the role of police in schools in practice.[364]

Of 683 police officers in British schools in 2021, 357 were employed by the Met in London. The Met and Avon and Somerset forces are reviewing their officers' roles in schools, after legal challenges that they discriminate against pupils of colour.[365]

The disproportionality of black prisoners compared with white prisoners is greater in the UK than in the US. In the UK, black Caribbean children are three times more likely to be excluded from school than white pupils.[366]

Education becomes a place of inequality

Through education, pupils learn their place in the unequal hierarchy of work. Marxist principles indicate that social institutions act to serve the economic system. Going on from there, researchers claim schools get pupils ready for their expected work roles by organising social interaction and rewards for the individual to match the workplace environment.[367]

So, pupils from working class backgrounds are prepared in school by a process of conformity into accepting low-status jobs. Children of the elite, meanwhile, are encouraged to make individual decisions which ready them for jobs in which they are bosses rather than the bossed.[368]

The meritocratic system of qualifications tells pupils that if you succeed in education you deserve a job that makes you wealthy, while if you fail to get qualifications you should only expect to get a low-paid job, or perhaps involvement in offending behaviour. However, in the case of pupils of colour, if they are Muslim or black Caribbean, they see from outside society that work is hard, if not impossible, to acquire. Therefore, while the white working class still has job opportunities, Muslims and black Caribbeans are becoming an underclass to whom jobs are inaccessible.[369]

This pushing to the bottom of people, based on race, gender or class, creates problems of poverty which leads to tensions with other classes. The government manages these tensions through the welfare state, but also through the power of prisons.[370]

The growth of capitalist economies led to the need to manage workers so as to maximise profits. Disciplinary practices of surveillance used in prisons were extended to other institutions, such as factories, schools and hospitals. So, in the US and UK, social welfare and the criminal justice system are used to manage surplus labour that is poor and disadvantaged. These groups are considered potentially dangerous. So, putting them disproportionately into prison keeps people from considering what the real structural issues are that discriminate against these people.[371]

Discipline and educational exclusion

The most common reason for school exclusion is persistent disruptive behaviour. Middle-class cultural capital is the norm in schools. Pupils who display alternative cultural capital will be strongly discouraged and eventually punished.

Let's take hairstyles. Children in the UK are often prohibited from dyeing their hair 'unnatural' colours. In the US, black children's Afros are seen as a distraction in class. In the UK, children are prohibited from wearing their hair too short, from wearing patterns in their hair, and from wearing cornrows. The reason given is that there is a link between hairstyles and gangs. It seems that UK schools cannot distinguish between working class, black cultural norms and criminality. This is seen by black pupils as discrimination for having African hair. Discipline ranges from going to an internal exclusion unit to going home until the haircut grows out.[372]

The idea seems to be that if pupils have smart uniforms and move around the school quietly, discipline is being achieved. However, if working class, and, more noticeably, black bodies are moving, things don't look so disciplined. Add in the non-middle-class and non-white language forms that white people might associate with street culture, this might look like trouble to white teachers. That's before going into the classroom.

In the classroom incidents will be treated differently depending on the pupils and teachers involved. The Department for Education and Skills agreed that black pupils' behaviour would be more likely reprimanded than white pupils.'[373] This racism results from social conditioning that says that black pupils are threatening. In due course this can lead to black pupils being excluded for violent behaviour.

Exclusion statistics may mask the extent of the problem, since they don't include 'unofficial exclusion' (asking parents to withdraw their child voluntarily) and 'internal exclusion', in which pupils can be separated from the main school population.[374]

An over-focus on behaviour can result in pupils' academic ability being ignored. Pushing the pupil down into lower-ability sets can also result in them getting poorer grades.

'How does school relate to prison?'

Exclusion from school can make exclusion from society and offending more likely. Offending might include alcohol abuse, drug abuse and petty crime. If a pupil gets good qualifications that reduces the prospects of criminal activity. However, if a black pupil has poor qualifications, they can not only see poor job prospects ahead but negative stereotypes of black youth.[375]

Research in the UK has found that by age five to six, pupils can be identified as causing low-level disruption. Examples include speaking when asked to be quiet. Moving when asked to stay still. Not following teacher's instructions. This label sticks with the pupil and determines how teachers see them. The school's response includes moving pupils to a lower set. It also includes moving the pupil to a place physically separate from the classroom. If they then move, it is only with a staff escort. Falling behind educationally can result in a pupil being bullied. They are likely to respond to this with physical violence.

There are similarities with prison. In prison, inmates are kept isolated from other prisoners and do little meaningful activity. If they move around it is only with a staff escort. If they are offered education, it does not meet their needs. Their communal life in prison is with people whose experience is like their own, of school exclusion, social exclusion and offending.[376]

Non-teaching staff's role in school discipline

With the UK prison population growing in the last 20 years, it is not surprising if people ask if there's a school-to-prison pipeline in UK.

The government has given teachers powers to stop and search pupils for objects banned by school rules, such as mobile phones. They've also given schools powers to punish pupils for behaviour outside both school premises and school hours. Some rights at exclusion appeals have been denied.[377]

Following the murder of a head teacher by a pupil and amid fears about gang violence, there are now full-time police officers in many city schools.[378] Their initial work was to stop crime on school premises, keep teachers and pupils safe, and support staff with respect to discipline.[379]

However, these police roles have now been widened. They now include identifying factors that might point to bad or extremist behaviour in the future. These powers raise concerns. People need to take care that pupils don't feel discriminated against owing to their family background. Thinking pupils might offend in future is considered more likely to result in their delinquency. Teachers seeing black Caribbean males as potentially violent is then carried through to profiling them as criminals on the streets.[380]

Giving police officers the power to identify future gang members has been highlighted by the Police Foundation themselves as concerning. This can lead to the misuse of 'Joint Enterprise' law to justify longer prison sentences for men of colour.[381]

Conclusion

Schools, perhaps unwittingly, identify, isolate and 'train' a small minority of pupils to become the future imprisoned offender. Black Caribbean men are more likely than any other ethnic group to come into this category. Pupils that enter the schools-to-prison pipeline seem to have been prepared for imprisoning at least partly by negative schooling.

This might explain the high rate of repeat arrests for teenage offenders. To the re-offender, if through their reoffence, they succeed financially, their problems will all be solved. If they aren't successful, prison isn't so bad an experience, so they can get through that alright.[382]

Chapter Fourteen. Curriculum

Introduction

Teachers responding to a recent study saw the current curriculum in schools as too narrow and too white. The National Curriculum has been overhauled to herald a return to 'traditional' subjects and teaching methods which have sought to overturn decades of more diverse, socially inclusive and multicultural curricula.[383]

These changes include emphasising schools' responsibilities to promote fundamental British values. This follows on from their earlier responsibility for implementing the Prevent agenda. These responsibilities respond to a fear of extremist ideologies, terrorism and Islamic Sharia law. So, schools are now on the frontline of current religious wars. It seems that schools are now focusing on controlling pupils of colour, rather than educating them.[384]

People of colour's history omitted

Focusing on a version of British history that celebrates 'the distinguished role of these islands in the history of the world' has resulted not just in the teaching of black history being made optional, but in it being ignored and in practice omitted.[385]

Of 59 history GCSE modules available from the three largest exam boards (Edexcel, OCR and AQA), 12 specifically mention black history. Only five mention black people's history in Britain. So only 11 per cent of GCSE pupils in 2019 studied modules that referred to the contribution of black people to British history.[386]

The British Empire has been a very significant part of British history over the last 400 years. Yet only nine per cent of pupils studied modules that referred to the Empire.

Black people are often studied in the context of the slave trade. This can reinforce views of black people as victims. Black historians see the Empire and slave trade as part of the imperialists' history. The black history of this period they see as the tremendous number of rebellions and Maroon societies, the Haitian Revolution, Marcus Garvey and the Universal Negro Improvement Association, and the Pan-African congresses.[387]

The real era of African independence was the time before European conquests and enslavement, and not the period since 1957, so this period before European conquest is inspirational for people of colour to learn.[388] In 2019, one-third of GCSE pupils took modules focused on non-European or American cultures. Of these, 95 per cent studied one of the two modules on China at the time of Mao Zedong. Three modules focused on non-European or American culture that was not in the context of an invasion: the Mughal Empire 1526–1707; South Africa 1960–94 and Middle East conflict 1945–95. However, less than two per cent of pupils studied these last three modules at GCSE level.

As a result of not learning about people of colour's history in Britain, white people aren't aware of many people of colour's contribution to Britain. Further, many white people don't understand many people of colour and how they think. People of colour don't see themselves in the people they learn about in history, so don't understand who they themselves are or who their role models should be. They feel they don't belong in Britain and that people of colour have not made a contribution to Britain.

Curriculum violence

This results when pupils are asked to do a staged re-enactment of an event so as to understand black history. For example, giving a pupil a cotton plant and their finding how difficult it is to pick cotton; pretending to be a KKK member and justifying your treatment of black people; a plantation owner calling a black pupil their slave. What the pupil of colour feels is emotional destruction and trauma, legitimised as teaching. Instead, pupils need to learn critical skills to engage with difficult histories.[389]

Some suggested ways forward

To avoid running into time pressures caused by GCSE exams, researchers found that it would be best to address race and ethnicity during pupils' first two years at secondary school. Another big opportunity to address race and ethnicity is in school assemblies, in any year.[390]

While also embedding issues of race, ethnicity, gender, class, disability and sexuality in schooling structures, researchers suggest schools should move to an anti-racist curriculum. This could be implemented by racially literate teachers. Such a curriculum could demonstrate that, for example, modernity is shaped by racism, white supremacy and coloniality. This could be shown in history by focusing on anti-colonial resistance movements. Or in English by reading a more diverse range of authors, such as Malorie Blackman, Bernardine Evaristo, Candice Carty-Williams, Zadie Smith and Alex Wheatle.

Pupils' focus could be moved on from seeing racism in terms of individual acts to considering structural racism.[391] This might help white pupils identify the effects of their whiteness and the operation and domination of their white, structurally embedded advantage. Pupils of colour could study content preparing them for life in a society that is racist.

Such changes might be constrained by exam boards being heavily white and by current resources and textbooks perpetuating racist stereotypes.

Case study: migration, belonging and Empire

The DfE recognises 'how people's lives have shaped this nation and how Britain has influenced and been influenced by the wider world'. It calls for pupils to be taught 'tolerance' as part of fundamental British values 'by enabling pupils to acquire an appreciation of and respect for their own and other cultures'.[392]

At Key Stages 3 and 4 (GCSE level) migration, belonging and empire can be and is being taught as a part of the history and

English curricula. However, this depends on the modules, topics and texts that schools select.

Around four per cent of pupils taking History GCSE are taking the 'Migration to Britain' option (also contains some empire) under exam boards OCR and AQA. This level of take-up being the case, migration, belonging and empire should be followed at Key Stage 3 across different disciplines.

People don't know how many schools are taking this course. Academies do not have to follow the National Curriculum. A convincing case should be made to academy chains to cover this course as part of their own curriculum.

Research is required to find out how many schools are delivering migration, belonging and empire, and to find out what is being delivered and what is being left out. An assessment should be made of pupils' knowledge of the course and of teachers' interest in it and concerns. Government should carry out this research and update the curriculum in line with its findings.

A survey of teachers found that 78 per cent wanted training for teaching migration and 71 per cent wanted training for teaching empire. ITE courses do not have the time to help teachers teach controversial issues.

UCL's Centre for Holocaust Education provides a good benchmark for a programme for supporting teachers of migration, belonging and empire. It provides an ITE programme nationally for starter teachers, together with online resources, CPD days and an accredited master's online course. In 2018/19, 70 per cent of pupils in classes given by teachers who had attended the CPD were able to answer correctly core knowledge questions about the Holocaust.

Future CPD should both engage with higher educators and with experienced teachers of migration, belonging and empire. Government should therefore fund an ITE and CPD programme on migration, belonging and empire in conjunction with universities.[393]

Some further suggested resources for teachers

Ages
4–7
Ganeri, A. (2018). *Questions and feelings about racism*. London: Franklin Watts.
5–6
Smith, D. (2016). *Unique and wonderful*. CreateSpace.
Harrison, V. (2018). *Bold women in black history*. London: Puffin.
6–11
Hewitt, S. (2011). *How can I deal with racism?* London: Franklin Watts.
Wilson, J. (2018). *Young, gifted and black*. London: Quarto Publishing PLC.
7–9
Lacey, J. (2017). *Dealing with racism*. London: Franklin Watts.
7–16
Williams, M. (1999–2018). *Black scientists and inventors*, books 1–8. London: BIS.
Williams, M. (2007). *Black women scientists and inventors*, book 1.
Williams, M. (2017). *Blacks in Mathematics and Science*, workbooks 1–2.
10–13
Heuchan, C. and Shukla, N. (2020). *What is race? Who are racists? Why does skin colour matter? And other big questions*. London: Wayland.

12 and above
Lyndon, D. (2010) *African Empires*. London: Franklin Watts. BCE to 16th century CE.
Africa and the slave trade. 15th–19th century.
Resistance and abolition. 15th–19th century.
Civil rights and equality. 20th century.
Arts and music. 19th–20th century.
Community and identity. 20th century.
Adi, H. (1995) *The history of the African and Caribbean communities in Britain*. 16th–20th centuries. London: Hodder Wayland.
Walker, R. et al. (2017) *Black British history: black influences on British culture (1948 to 2016)*. London: Reklaw Education Ltd and Croydon Suppl. Education Project.

Walker, R. (2019) *Black history matters*. BCE–20th century. London: Franklin Watts.

14 and above
Spafford, M. et al. (2017) *OCR GCSE History Explaining the modern world: Migration, empire and the historic environment.*
Mohamud, A. and Whitburn. R. (2016) *AQA GCSE History. Migration, empires and the people.*
Mohamud, A. and Whitburn. R. (2016) *Doing justice to history: transforming black history in secondary schools.* London: UCL IOE Press. 11th, 14th–16th, 18th–20th centuries.
Harriott, J. (1992). *Black women in Britain.* London: B.T. Batsford Ltd. 20th century.

General
Kaufmann, M. (2017) *Black Tudors.* London: Oneworld. 16th century.
Chater, K. (2009) *Untold histories.* Manchester: Manchester University Press. 17th–18th century.
Vernon, P. and Osborne, A. (2020) *100 Great Black Britons.* London: Robinson. 1 16th century, 14 18–19th century, 85 20th century.

Websites
blackhistory4schools.com
justice2history.org
blackhistoryman.com

REFERENCES

1 Konan. (2019). Music saved my life. Banning drill takes hope away from black British kids like me. *The Guardian*. 13 June.

2 Orwell, G. (1937, rprtd. 2001). *The road to Wigan pier*, p. 153. London: Penguin; Moore, D. (2020). Orwell's Scottish ancestry and slavery. *George Orwell Studies*, Volume 5, No. 1; *Legacies of British Slave-Ownership Database*, Centre for the Study of the Legacies of British Slave-Ownership, University College London. Available online at http://wwwdepts-live.ucl.ac.uk/lbs/estate/view/2830; Cork, T. (2018). Taxpayers in Bristol were still paying debt to city's slave owners in 2015, Treasury admits. *BristolLive*. 13 February.

3 Dodd, V. (2019). Children whitening skin to avoid racial hate crime, charity finds. *The Guardian*. 30 May.

4 Hart, A. (2014). *That's racist: how the regulation of speech and thought divides us all*. Exeter: Imprint Academic.

5 Number Cruncher Politics. (2020). For the ITV programme 'Stephen Lawrence: has Britain changed?' Poll of 3065 adults. https://www.ncpolitics.uk/2020/07/stephen-lawrence-has-britain-changed/#:~:text=For%20ITV%E2%80%99s%20programme%20%E2%80%9CStephen%20Lawrence%3A%20Has%20Britain%20Changed%3F%E2%80%9D%2C,subsample%2C%20enables%20proper%20analysis%20of%20non-white%20Britons%E2%80%99%20views

6 Hegel, G. W. F. (1807, rprtd 1977). *Phenomenology of spirit*, paras 178–96, pp. 111–9. Trans. Miller, A. V. Oxford: OUP.

7 Wollstonecraft, M. (1975). *A vindication of the rights of women*, Poston, C. H., ed., pp. 23, 34, 56, 61, 147, 152. New York, NY: W. W. Norton.

8 A term increasingly used in Britain for people who are racialised as 'other than white', that is, African, Asian, Latin American and Pacific Islander people. Chetty, D. (2016). 'You can't say that! Stories have to be about white people'. In Shukla, N., ed., *The good immigrant*, p. 97. London: Unbound.

9 Richardson, J. E. and Wodak, R. (2009). The impact of visual racism, pp. 61–9. *Controversia*, 6(2): 45–77.

10 Chodorow, N. J. (1978). *The reproduction of mothering*, pp. 58–76. Berkeley, CA: University of California Press.

11 de Beauvoir, S. (1989). *The Second Sex*, pp. xxii–xxiv. New York, NY: Vintage Books.

12 Cottrell, S. (2017). *Critical thinking skills*, third edition, pp. 187–210. London: Red Globe Press.

13 Gopal, P. (2019b). If we can't call racism by its name, diversity will remain a meaningless buzzword. *The Guardian*. 8 October; Haley, A. (1974, rprtd. 1991). *Roots*, p. 293. London: Vintage.

14 Colley, L. (2003). *Britons: forging the nation, 1707–1837*. London: Pimlico.

15 Gopal, P. (2019a). *Insurgent empire: anticolonial resistance and British dissent*, pp. 5, 9, 14–22. London: Verso.

16 Du Bois, W. E. B. (1903, rprtd.1994). *The souls of black folk*, pp. 1–3. Mineola, NY: Dover Thrift Edition.

17 Cugoano, O. (1787). *Thoughts and Sentiments on the Evil and Wicked Traffic of the Slavery and Commerce of the Human Species*. London; Morrison, T. (1992). *Playing in the dark: whiteness and the literary imagination*, pp. 4–5, 11–2. Cambridge, MA: Harvard University Press.

18 *Education pack*. (2013). EAH Consequences. www.eahconsequences.com

19 Simpson, D. (1993). *Romanticism, nationalism and the revolt against theory*, pp. 64–103. Chicago, IL: University of Chicago Press.

20 Mance, H. (2016). Britain has had enough of experts, says Gove. *Financial Times*. 3 June.

21 Alibhai Brown, Y. (2000). *Who do we think we are?* pp. 117, 121, 155–6. London: Allen Lane.

22 Collins, P. H. (1998). *Fighting words*, pp. 201–28. Minneapolis, MN: University of Minneapolis Press.

23 Sandhu, B. (2017). *The value of lived experience in social change*, p. 5. http://livedexperience.org/wp=content/uploads/2017/07/The-Lived-Experience-Baljeet-Sandhu-VLE-full-report.pdf.

24 Crenshaw, K. (1991). Mapping the margins: intersectionality, identity politics and violence against women of color. *Stanford Law Review* 43: 1241–99.

25 Davis, A. Y. (2011). *Women, culture and politics*, pp. 30–1. New York, NY: Vintage Books.

26 Dabashi, H. (2015). *Can non-Europeans think?* p. xii. London: Zed Books.

27 Berry, D. (2016). What happens when white men realize that their perspective isn't the only one that matters? *National Post*, 29 July; Ani, M. (1994). *Yurugu: an African-centered critique of European cultural thought and behavior*, pp. 311–35, 511–552. Trenton, NJ: Africa World Press.

28 Mahbubani, K. (2008). *The new Asian hemisphere*. New York, NY: Public Affairs.

29 Gundara, J. S. (2000). *Interculturalism education and inclusion*, pp. 1–22. London: Paul Chapman Publishing.

30 Mamdani, M. (2004). *Good Muslim, Bad Muslim: America, the Cold War and the Roots of Terror*. New York, NY: Pantheon Books; Mamdani, M. (2009). *Saviors and Survivors: Darfur, Politics and the war on Terror*. New York, NY: Pantheon Books.

31 Asafu-Adjaye. N. (2015). *Melanin monologues: a Black British perspective*, pp. 16–7. London: The Wordsmiths Workshop Limited.

32 Choudry, S. (2021). *Equitable education*, p. 211. St. Albans: Critical Publishing; Dulin-Keita et al. (2011). The defining moment: children's conceptualization of race and experiences with racial discrimination. E*thnic and Racial Studies*, 34(4): 662–682.

33 E.g., Bhavnani, R., et al. (2005). *Tackling the roots of racism*, pp. 7–21. Bristol: Policy Press.

34 Gomes Eanes de Zurara (1896, rprtd. 2016). *Chronicle of the Discovery and Conquest of Guinea*, 2 vols, eds. Beazley and Prestage, chs. XIV, XV and XVIII. London: Hakluyt Society.

35 Kendi, I. X. (2017). *Stamped from the beginning: the definitive history of racist ideas in America*, pp. 5, 20–1, 23. London: The Bodley Head.

36 Martinez, M. E. (2008). *Genealogical fictions: Limpieza de Sangre, religion and gender in colonial Mexico*, p. 33, 34. Stanford, CA: Stanford University Press; Greer, M. R. et. al, eds. (2007). *Rereading the Black Legend*, pp. 2, 12–14, 314–321. Chicago, IL: University of Chicago Press; Vinson III, B. (2018). *Before Mestizaje*, p. 13. New York, NY: CUP.

37 Mos-Shogbamimu, S. (2021). *This is why I resist*, p. 9. London: Headline.

38 Bhavnani, R. et al. (2005). *Op. cit.*, p. 8.

39 Keita, M. (2000). *Race and the writing of history*, p. 8. Oxford: OUP.

40 Wells, S. (2007). *Deep ancestry: inside the Genographic Project*, p. 40. Washington, DC: National Geographic.

41 Jablonski, N. G. (2012). *Living color: the biological and social meaning of skin color*, pp. 27–8, 53. Berkeley, CA: University of California Press.

42 Hiernaux, J., ed., (1965). Biological aspects of race. *International Social Science Journal*, xvii (i): 71–161.

43 Oxford Dictionaries. Social construct. OUP. https://en.oxforddictionaries.com/definition/social_construct

44 Khan Academy. Social constructionism. https://www.khanacademy.org/test-prep/mcat/society-and-culture/social-structures/v/social-constructionism

45 Delgado, R. and Stefancic, J. (2017). *Critical race theory*, p. 9. New York, NY: New York UP.

46 Lentin, A. (2020). Coronavirus is the ultimate demonstration of the real-world impact of racism. *The Guardian*. 12 May.

47 Hylton, K. (2018). *Contesting 'race' and sport*, p. 2. Abingdon: Routledge; Du Bois, W. E. B. (1903, rprtd. 1994). *Op. cit.*, p. 9.

48 Delgado, R. and Stefancic, J. (2017). *Op. cit.*, p. 182.

49 Miles, R. and Brown, M. (2003). *Racism*. Second edition, pp. 4–6. London: Routledge.

50 Robinson, C. (1983). *Black Marxism*, pp. 185–301. London: Zed Press.

51 S. Sayyid. (2004). Slippery people: the immigrant imaginary and the grammar of colour. In Law, I. et al., eds., *Institutional racism in higher education*. London: Trentham Books.

52 Peller, G. (1990). Race Consciousness. *Duke Law Journal*. Vol. 1990: 758–847.

53 Hirsch, A. (2009). Watchdog split over Trevor Phillips leadership and remit, *The Guardian*, 20 July.

54 Crenshaw, K. W. (1988). Race, Reform and Retrenchment: Transformation and Legitimation in Antidiscrimination Law. *Harvard Law Review*. Vol. 101, No. 7 (May 1988), pp. 1331–1387.

55 Andrews, K. (2013). *Resisting racism*, pp. 22–3. London: Institute of Education.

56 Oluo, I. (2018). *So you want to talk about race*, pp. 8–11, 24–6, 30–6. New York, NY: Hachette.

57 Oluo, I. (2018). *Ibid.*, pp. 14–22.

58 Kendi, I. X. (2017). *Op. cit.*, pp. 5, 20–1, 23.

59 Coates, T.-N. (2015). *Between the world and me*, p. 7. Melbourne: The Text Publishing Company.

60 Oluo, I. (2018). *Op. cit.*, pp. 11–14.

61 Harnden, T. (2009). Barack Obama gets 30 death threats a day, stretching US Secret Service. *The Telegraph*. 3 August.

62 Asafu-Adjaye, N. (2015). *Op. cit.*, pp. 11–12. London: The Wordsmiths Workshop Limited.

63 Bhavnani, R. et al. (2005). *Op. cit.*, p. 11.

64 Mirza, H. S. (2005). The more things change, the more they stay the same, in Richardson, B., ed., *Tell it like it is: how our schools fail Black children*, p. 116. London/Stoke-on-Trent: Bookmarks/Trentham Books.

65 Bhavnani, R. et al. (2005). *Op. cit.*, p. 11–2.

66 Essed, P. (1990). *Everyday racism*, pp. 12–18. Trans. Jaffe, C. Alameda, CA: Hunter House.

67 Delgado, R. and Stefancic, J. (2017). *Op. cit.*, p. 183.

68 Fredman, S., ed., (2001). *Discrimination and human rights*, p. 2. Oxford: OUP.

69 Mirza, H. and Meetoo. V. (2012). *Respecting difference*, pp. 4–5. London: Institute of Education.

70 Younge, G. (2002). Churchill – the truth. *The Guardian*. 30 September.

71 Kilcup, K. (2000). *Native American women's writing 1800–1924*. Oxford: Blackwell.

72 Mutwa, V. C. (1998). *Indaba my children*. Edinburgh: Payback Press.

73 Correll, J. et al. (2002). The police officer's dilemma: using ethnicity to disambiguate potentially threatening individuals. *Journal of Personality and Social Psychology, 83,* 1314–1329; Banaji, M. R. and Greenwald, A. G. (2013). *Blindspot*, pp. 71–122. New York, NY: Delacorte Press.

74 Andrews, K. (2013). *Op. cit.*, pp. 22–4.

75 Rafiq, R. (2019). Not *just* a Black Muslim Woman, pp. 199–208. In M. Khan, ed., *It's not about the burqa*. London: Picador.

76 Crenshaw, K. (1989). Demarginalizing the intersection of race and sex: a black feminist critique of antidiscrimination doctrine, feminist theory and antiracist politics. *University of Chicago Legal Forum*: Vol. 1989: Iss. 1, Article 8. Available at: http://chicagounbound.uchicago.edu/uclf/vol1989/iss1/8

77 Collins, P. H. and Bilge, S. (2016). *Intersectionality*, pp. 1–31. Cambridge: Polity Press; Hancock, A.-M. (2016). *Intersectionality: an intellectual history*. New York, NY: OUP.

78 Essed, P. (1990). *Op. cit.*, p. 24.

79 Mos-Shogbamimu, S. (2021). *Op. cit.*, p. 6.

80 Premack, R. (2018). *14 things people think are fine to say at work – but actually are racist, sexist or offensive.* http://uk.businessinsider.com/microaggression-unconscious-bias-at-work-2018–6; Reid, S. (2018). How to deal with microaggressions as a black woman, *The Guardian*, 13 August.

81 Sue, D. W. (2010). *Microaggressions in everyday life*, p. xvi. Hoboken, NJ: Wiley.

82 Sue, D. W. (2010). *Racial microaggressions in everyday life.* https://www.psychologytoday.com/gb/blog/microaggressions-in-everyday-life/201010/racial-microaggressions-in-everyday-life

83 Gopal, P. (2019b). *Op. cit.*

84 Akala. (2018). *Natives: race and class in the ruins of empire*, p. 34. London: Two Roads.

85 *Oxford English Dictionary*, 2nd edition. (1989). Oxford: OUP.

86 Dalal, F. (2002). *Race, colour and the processes of racialization*, pp. 135–170. Hove: Routledge.

87 Younge, G. (1999). *No place like home*, p. 39. London: Picador.

88 Rankin, L. (2013). Colorblindness is the new racism. *MIC.* https://www.mic.com/articles/55867/colorblindness-is-the-new-racism

89 US - Leonardo, Z. (2009). *Race, whiteness and education*, pp. 130–4. London: Routledge; Britain – Khan, O. (2016). *Colourblindness fails to deliver race equality.* http://www.runnymedetrust.org/blog/cerd-reflections; Europe, Latin America, Caribbean – Bonilla-Silva, E. (2014). *Racism without racists*, pp. 232, 245. Lanham, MD: Rowman & Littlefield.

90 Rose, T. (2015). *How structural racism works.* 7:36. 21 December. https://www.youtube.com/watch?v=T5b3DJMBmic

91 Carr, S. (2017). #AndABlackWomanAtThat: a discussion of power and privilege. *Red Pepper*, 9 March. http://www.redpepper.org.uk/andablackwomanatthat-a-discussion-of-power-and-privilege/

92 Eddo-Lodge, R. (2017). *Why I'm no longer talking to white people about race*, pp. 66–72, 81–4. London: Bloomsbury Circus; Khan, O. (2017). The silent cleansing of black men from society. *Huffington Post, UK.* 27 June.

93 Shaw, B. et al. (2016). *Ethnicity, gender and social mobility.* London: Social Mobility Commission; Equality and Human Rights Commission. (2016). *Healing a divided Britain.* London: EHRC.

94 Dept. for Education. (2021). *Development goals for 4 to 5 year olds, 2018/19.* 4 March. https://www.ethnicity-facts-figures.service.gov.uk/education-skills-and-training/early-years/attainment-of-development-goals-by-children-aged-4-to-5-years/latest#full-page-history

95 Social Mobility Commission. (2016). *Asian Muslims and black people do better in school, worse in work.* 28 December. https://www.gov.uk/government/news/asian-muslims-and-black-people-do-better-in-school-worse-in-work data at Shaw, B. et al. (2016). *Op. cit.*; Centre

for Market and Public Organization (Burgess, S. and Greaves, E.). (2009). *Test scores, subjective assessment of ethnic minorities*. Working paper no. 09/221.

96 McIntyre, N., Parveen N. and Thomas, T. (2021). Exclusion rates five times higher for black Caribbean pupils in parts of England. *The Guardian*. 24 March; Dept. for Education. (2021). *Permanent exclusions by ethnicity, 2018/19*. 24 February. https://www.ethnicity-facts-figures.service.gov.uk/education-skills-and-training/absence-and-exclusions/permanent-exclusions/latest#:~:text=Permanent%20Exclusion%20rate,%20and%20number%20of%20permanent%20exclusions,,%20%20215%20%2019%20more%20rows

97 Amnesty International. (2018). *Trapped in the matrix*. https://www.amnesty.org.uk/files/reports/Trapped%20in%20the%20Matrix%20Amnesty%20report.pdf.

98 ONS. (2021). *Homicide in England and Wales, 2019/20*. 25 February. https://www.ons.gov.uk/peoplepopulationandcommunity/crimeandjustice/articles/homicideinenglandandwales/yearendingmarch2020/#main-points

99 19.8 per cent of black people, compared with 17.4 per cent of Asian people. Ministry of Housing, Communities and Local Government. (2020). *Most income-deprived 10 per cent of neighbourhoods, by ethnicity, English indices of deprivation, 2019*. 30 September. https://www.ethnicity-facts-figures.service.gov.uk/uk-population-by-ethnicity/demographics/people-living-in-deprived-neighbourhoods/latest; Wilson, A. (2020). *In black and white*, pp. 4–7. London: Endeavour

100 Osei-West, D. (2021). *Racial disparities in higher education*. https://www.birmingham.ac.uk/schools/social-policy/social-policy-matters/news/2021/july-issue/racial-disparities-in-higher-education; HESA data for 2016/17. Cited in Byrne, B., et al., eds. (2018). *Ethnicity, race and inequality in the UK*, pp. 116–8. Bristol: Policy Press

101 HESA Student Record. (2021). *UK undergraduate degree results, 2019/20*. 2 August. https://www.ethnicity-facts-figures.service.gov.uk/education-skills-and-training/higher-education/undergraduate-degree-results/latest

102 HESA staff record, 2017–18. Cited in Universities UK (2019). *Black, Asian and minority ethnic pupil attainment at UK universities*, p. 15. London: Universities UK.

103 Wood, M. et al. (2009). *A test for racial discrimination in recruitment practice in British cities*. National Centre for Social Research for Department for Work and Pensions. Research report no. 607. Norwich: HMSO.

104 Jivraj, S. and Simpson, L. (2015). *Ethnic identity and inequalities in Britain*, p. 161. Bristol: Policy Press.

105 Runnymede Trust. (2014). *End racism this generation*, survey in evaluation report, May, p. 4. http://www.runnymedetrust.org/end-racism/wp-content/uploads/Final_End_Racism_This_Generation_Evaluation_Report_May_2014.pdf

106 Home Office. (2021). *Stop and search, England and Wales, 2019/20.* 22 February. https://ethnicity-facts-figures.service.gov.uk/crime-justice-and-the-law/policing/stop-and-search/latest?fbclid=lwAR2EIRhzH2YCdN8WOMbSTug94PHsiz7mAr8wyBLdRBYTGi_yS-bE1JTmKy4

107 Home Office. (2020). *Number of arrests by ethnicity, 2018/19.* 17 September. https://www.ethnicity-facts-figures.service.gov.uk/crime-justice-and-the-law/policing/number-of-arrests/latest#:~:text=Arrest%20rate%20per%201,000%20people%20and%20number%20of%20%208,527%20%2019%20more%20rows

108 ONS. (2020). Coronavirus and the social impacts on different ethnic groups in the UK. 14 December. https://www.ons.gov.uk/peoplepopulationandcommunity/culturalidentity/ethnicity/articles/coronavirusandthesocialimpactsondifferentethnicgroupsintheUK/2020; Inman, P. (2020). BAME groups hit by Covid 'triple whammy' official UK study finds. *The Guardian.* 14 December.

109 Dupont, C. R. (2014). *Mississippi praying*, pp. 16–7. New York, NY: New York UP.

110 Andrews, K. (2018). *Back to Black*, pp. 283–4. London: Zed.

111 Kendi, I. X. (2016). *Stamped from the beginning*, p. 10. London: The Bodley Head.

112 Lindsay, B. (2019). *We need to talk about race*, pp. 11-3. London: SPCK; Nakrani, S. (2019). John Barnes: 'I was seen as the voice of reason on race. I haven't changed'. *The Guardian.* 14 October; Oluo, I. (2018). *Op. cit.*, pp. 26–36.

113 Fryer, P. (1984). *Staying power*, pp. 133–90. London: Pluto.

114 Eddo-Lodge, R. (2017). *Op. cit.*, pp. 81–4, 208. London: Bloomsbury Circus.

115 Saad, L. F. (2020). *Me and white supremacy*, pp. 40–5, 53–9, 148–54. London: Quercus.

116 Gopal, P. (2019b). *Op. cit.*

117 Mills, C. W. (1997). *The racial contract*, p. 1. Ithaca, NY: Cornell UP.

118 Ansley, F. L. (1989). "Stirring the Ashes: Race, Class and the Future of Civil Rights Scholarship". Cornell Law Review. **74**: 993ff; Gopal, P. (2019b). *Op. cit;* Saad, L. F. (2020). *Op. cit.*, p. 12.

119 Wilson, A. N. (1990). *Black-on-black violence*, pp. xiii-xx. Bronx, NY: Afrikan World InfoSystems.

120 Glaude Jr., E. S. (2016). *Democracy in black*, pp. 30–1. New York, NY: Crown Publishers.

121 Abdi, M. (2021). *Language is important: Why we are moving away from the terms 'allyship' and 'privilege' in our work*. 14 June. https://ma-consultancy.co.uk/blog/language-is-important-why-we-will-no-longer-use-allyship-and-privilege-in-our-work

122 Shilliam, R. (2018). *Race and the undeserving poor*, pp. 4, 159–81. Newcastle: Agenda.

123 Eddo-Lodge, R. (2017). *Op. cit.*, p. 87.

124 The anti-racist educator. (2020). *White Privilege Test*, 3 July https://drive.google.com/file/d/1i4UDPSO2L6z_9gfrptSSTBTpEgvkgBSA/view; McIntosh, P. (1990). White privilege and male privilege, pp. 2–5. *Independent School*, Winter issue.

125 Fryer, P. (1993). *Black people in the British Empire*, p. 3. London: Pluto Classic.

126 Manjapra, K. (2020). *Colonialism in global perspective*, pp. 7–11. Cambridge: CUP; Nkrumah, K. (1965). *Neo-colonialism: the last stage of imperialism*, p. 8. London: Thomas Nelson and Sons Ltd.

127 Quijano, A. (1999). Coloniality and Modernity/Rationality. Trans. S. Therborn. In Therborn, G., ed., Globalizations and modernities: experiences, perspectives and Latin America. Stockholm, *FRN-Report*, 99: 5, 1.

128 Traynor, L. and Wilkinson, G. (2019). Boy, 11, gets called a 'slave' and the N-word by racist classmates. *Liverpool Echo*. 29/5 https://www.liverpoolecho.co.uk/news/liverpool-news/boy-11-gets-called-slave-16345721

129 Simien, J. (2014). *Dear white people*, p. 24. New York, NY: Atria Books.

130 Dictionary. (1966). *The Random House Dictionary of the English Language – the Unabridged Edition*. New York, NY: Random House.

131 Eddo-Lodge, R. (2017). *Op. cit.*, pp. 88–91, 95, 97, 202–3; Gopal, P. (2019b). *Op. cit.*

132 Gates Jr., H. L. (1988 rprtd. 2014). *The Signifying Monkey*, p. xii. New York, NY: OUP USA.

133 Olaleye, F. (2019). Talk of 'anti-white sentiment' distracts from the fight against institutional racism. *The Guardian.* 28 October; Eddo-Lodge, R. (2017). *Op. cit.*, p. 89.

134 CBS News. (2005). *60 minutes*, Mike Wallace interview with Morgan Freeman. http://www.cbsnews.com/video/watch/?id=1131418n, quoted on Snopes 2015.

135 Akala. (2018). *Op. cit.*, p. 24.

136 Cole, D. (2020). *The skin we're in: a year of black resistance and power.* Doubleday Canada; DeVos, T. and Banaji, M. R. (2005). American = White? *Journal of Personality and Social Psychology, 88,* 447–466.

137 Gopal, P. (2019b). *Op. cit.*

138 BBC. (2011). *Newsnight*, interview with David Starkey and others. YouTube, 14 August. https://www.youtube.com/watch?time_continue=2&v=OVq2bs8M9HM

139 O'Connor, C. (2013). *Playing the race card: a chip on my shoulder*, pp. 41–5. Self-published.

140 Akala. (2018). *Op. cit.*, p. 25.

141 Solow, B. L. (2014). *The economic consequences of the Atlantic Slave Trade*, p. 17. Lanham, MD: Rowman & Littlefield.

142 Hall, C. et al. (2014). *Legacies of British slave-ownership: colonial slavery and the formation of Victorian Britain*, p. 284. Cambridge: CUP.

143 Mason, R. (2015). Jamaica should 'move on from painful legacy of slavery' says Cameron. *The Guardian.* 30 September.

144 Davies, C. (2015). How do we know David Cameron has slave owners in family background? *The Guardian.* 29 September.

145 Newton, J. (2015). Did your ancestors own slaves? *MailOnline*, 17 November. http://www.dailymail.co.uk/news/article-3158078/The-Camerons-Benedict-Cumberbatch-Ben-Affleck-not-ones-related-slave-owners-Files-46-000-Brits-involved-evil-trade.html

146 HM Treasury. (2018). *Freedom of Information Act 2000: Slavery Abolition Act 1833.* 31 January. https://assets.publishing.service.gov.uk/government/uploads/system/uploads/attachment_data/file/680456/FOI2018-00186_-_Slavery_Abolition_Act_1833_-_pdf_for_disclosure_log__003_.pdf

147 Akala. (2018). *Op. cit.*, pp. 25–6.

148 *Ibid.*, pp. 26–8.

149 Dahlgreen, W. (2014) The British Empire is 'something to be proud of'. *YouGov.* 26 July. https://yougov.co.uk/news/2014/07/26/britain-proud-its-empire/

150 Troesken, W. (2004). *Water, race and disease.* Cambridge, MA: MIT Press.
151 Phimister, I. (1988). *An economic and social history of Zimbabwe, 1890–1948*, p. 261. London: Longman.
152 Heldring, L. and Robinson, J. A. (2012). *Colonialism and economic development in Africa.* Working paper 18566. Cambridge, MA: National Bureau of Economic Research; Rodney, W. (1989). *How Europe underdeveloped Africa*, p. 225. Nairobi: East African Educational Publishers.
153 McQuade, J. (2017). Colonialism was a disaster and the facts prove it. *The Conversation.* 27 September; Davis, M. (2001). *Late Victorian holocausts: El Nino famines and the making of the Third World.* London: Verso.
154 Beer, M. (1921, rprtd 2010). *A history of British socialism V2, Part 3*, pp. 190–9. Whitefish, MT: Kessinger Legacy Reprints.
155 Akala. (2018). *Op. cit.*, pp. 28–9.
156 Morrison, T. (1992). *Playing in the dark: whiteness and the literary imagination*, pp. 11, 90. Cambridge, MA: Harvard UP.
157 Stokel-Walker, C. (2020). Ibram X. Kendi: "The status quo *is* racism." 30 October. https://www.esquire.com/uk/culture/books/a34522855/ibram-x-kendi-be-an-antiracist-interview/
158 Helms, J. E. and Cook, D. A. (1999). *Using race and culture in counseling and psychotherapy*, pp. 89–93. Needham Heights, MA: Allyn & Bacon.
159 Thandeka. (1999). *Learning to be white*, pp. 1–19. New York, NY: Continuum.
160 McIntosh, P. (1990). White privilege: unpacking the invisible knapsack. *Independent School.* Winter.
161 Eddo-Lodge. (2017). *Op. cit.*, pp. 86–7, 91–3.
162 Riggs, Marlon. (1986). *Ethnic notions.* San Francisco: Resolution/California Newsreel. Loaded to YouTube by Dazie Grego. (2021). 12th July. https://www.youtube.com/watch?v=9wCNYT0FRiY
163 Wilshaw, D. (2016). BBC4 TimeShift: Black and White Minstrels Show. https://www.youtube.com/watch?v=h8uZ6o6m_J0
164 Blackface! http://black-face.com/; Pickering, M. (2016). *Blackface minstrelsy in Britain.* Abingdon: Routledge.
165 Abercrombie, N. et al., eds. (1988). *The Penguin dictionary of sociology*, 2nd edition. Stereotypes. Harmondsworth: Penguin.
166 Gilman, Sander L. (1985). *Difference and pathology*, pp. 16–21. Ithaca, NY: Cornell UP.

167 Adichie, C. N. (2009). *The danger of a single story.* TED Global. https://www.ted.com/talks/chimamanda_adichie_the_danger_of_a_single_story
168 Katz, J. H. (1978, rprtd. 1989). *White awareness*, pp. 135–65, 193–5. Norman, OK: University of Oklahoma Press.
169 Dabiri, E. (2021). *What white people can do next: from allyship to coalition*, pp. 3–27. London: Penguin.
170 Irving, D. (2018). *Waking up white.* Cambridge, MA: Elephant Room Press; Battalora, J. (2013). *Birth of a white nation.* Houston, TX: Strategic books publishing and rights co.; Okun, T. (2010). *The emperor has no clothes.* Charlotte, NC: IAP; Thompson, B. and Tyagi, S. (1996). *Names we call home.* New York, NY: Routledge; Segrest, M. (1994). *Memoir of a race traitor.* Boston, MA: South End Press; Stalvey, L. M. (1989). *The education of a WASP.* Madison, WI: University of Wisconsin Press.
171 Malcolm X., Haley, A. (1965, rprtd. 2001). *The autobiography of Malcolm X*, pp. 494–6. London: Penguin.
172 Tatum, B. D. (2017). *Why are all the black kids sitting together in the cafeteria?* Twentieth anniversary edition, pp. 188–208. New York, NY: Basic Books.
173 Dabiri, E. (2021). *Op. cit.*, pp. 3–27; Ware, V. and L. Back. (2002). *Out of whiteness: color, politics and culture*, pp. 10, 13, 19, 140, 148–152. Chicago, IL: University of Chicago Press.
174 Malcolm X and Haley, A. (1965, rprtd. 2001). *Op. cit.*, pp. 495–6.
175 Anderson, J. (2012). A tension in the political thought of Huey P. Newton. *Journal of African-American Studies*, 16 (2), pp. 249–266.
176 Dabiri, E. (2021). *Op. cit.*, pp. 146–50.
177 Gillborn, D. (2008). *Racism and education: coincidence or conspiracy?* p. 192. Abingdon: Routledge.
178 Kivel, P. (2011). *Op. cit.*, pp. 142–6.
179 Van Dijk, T. A. (1993). *Elite discourse and racism*, pp. 8–9. Newbury Park, CA: Sage.
180 Emejulu, A. (2016). *Community development as micropolitics: comparing theories, policies and politics in America and Britain*, pp. 153–9. Bristol: Policy Press.
181 E.g., Ture, K. and Hamilton, C.V. (1967, rprtd. 1992). *Black Power: the politics of liberation in America*, pp. 49–64. New York, NY: Vintage.
182 Alinsky, S. D. (1962). *Rules for radicals.* New York, NY: Vintage.
183 Cooke, I. (1996). Whatever happened to the class of '68? The changing context of radical community work, pp. 8–12. In Cooke, I.

and Shaw, M., eds., *Radical community work: perspectives from practice in Scotland.* Edinburgh: Moray House.

184 Henry, W. L. (2007). *Whiteness made simple: stepping into the grey zone*, p. 39. London: Nu-Beyond Ltd.

185 George, M. P. (2013). *Whitewashed: unmasking the world of whiteness.* Dandelion Films. https://www.youtube.com/watch?v=rdaF_h06YX4

186 Asafu-Ajaye, N. (2015). *Op. cit.*, pp. 15–6.

187 Morrison, T. (1992). *Op. cit.*, pp. 11, 90. Cambridge, MA: Harvard UP.

188 Leonardo, Z. (2002). The souls of white folk. *Race, Ethnicity and Education*, 5(1), 29–50.

189 Bhopal, K. (2018). *White privilege*, p. 27. Bristol: Policy Press; The anti-racist educator (2019) https://www.theantiracisteducator.com/whiteness.

190 Frankenberg, R. (1993, rprtd. 1997). *The social construction of whiteness: white women, race matters*, p. 1. Minneapolis, MN: University of Minnesota.

191 Wise, T. (2007). Racism, white denial and the cost to white privilege. First three minutes. https://www.youtube.com/watch?v=mrA7ksL9sag

192 Tyler, K. (2012). *Whiteness, class and the legacies of empire*, pp. 14–15. Basingstoke: Palgrave Macmillan; Beckford, R. (2004). *God and the gangs*, pp. 74–81. London: Darton, Longman and Todd.

193 Feagin, J. R. (2013). *The white racial frame*, pp. x-xi, 1, 3, 9–22. Abingdon: Routledge.

194 Toure. (2015). White people explain why they feel oppressed. *Vice*, 18 September.

195 Media Reform Coalition. (2015). *Who owns the UK media?* http://www.mediareform.org.uk/wp-content/uploads/2015/10/Who_owns_the_UK_media-report_plus_appendix1.pdf

196 Hitchens, P. (1999). *The abolition of Britain*, pp. iii-xviii. London: Quartet.

197 Hitchens, P. (2012). Alien nation. *Mail on Sunday*, 15 December.

198 Taub, A. (2015). This browser hack reveals the truth about "political correctness". *Vox*. 10 August. https://www.vox.com/2015/8/10/9118339/political-correctness-respect

199 Frank, T. (2005). *What's the matter with Kansas?* pp. 13–17, 114–20. New York, NY: Henry Holt and Company.

200 Flying Rodent. (2011). Ban him? No, we need more of David Starkey's idiocy on TV. Comment no. 16. *Liberal Conspiracy*, 15

August. http://liberalconspiracy.org/2011/08/15/ban-him-no-we-need-more-of-david-starkeys-idiocy-on-tv/

201 Shoard, C. (2018). Steve McQueen: 'I experience racism every day'. *The Guardian*, 20 December.

202 Mohdin, A. and L. Campbell. (2020). Young, British & Black. *The Guardian*. 29 July. https://www.theguardian.com/uk-news/ng-interactive/2020/jul/29/young-british-black-voices-behind-uk-anti-racism-protests-george-floyd#8

203 Hall, S. and Gieben, B. (1992). *Formations of modernity*, pp. 1–7. Cambridge: Polity Press/Open University.

204 e.g. Knowles, C. (2005). Making whiteness: British lifestyle migrants in Hong Kong, in Alexander, C and Knowles, C., eds., *Making race matter*, pp. 90–110. Basingstoke: Palgrave.; Clarke, S. and Garner, S. (2010). *Op. cit.*, p. 11. London: Pluto Press.

205 Lewis, M. (2005). *Asylum: understanding public attitudes*. London: IPPR.

206 For example, see Housing Net's online calculator https://www.housingnet.co.uk/housing_points_calculator

207 ONS. (2012). *Local authority housing statistics: 2011–2012* (local authority-owned stock and stock management). ONS.

208 Jeffers, S. and Hoggett, P. (1995). Like counting deckchairs on the Titanic: a study of institutional racism and housing allocations in Haringey and Lambeth. *Housing Studies*, 10 (3): 325–44.

209 Robinson. (2010). New immigrants and migrants in social housing in Britain, p. 71. *Policy & Politics*, 38 (1).

210 Flanders, S. (2010. Have British jobs gone to British workers? *BBC News*. 21 April.

211 Dustmann, C. and Frattini, T. (2013). *The fiscal effects of immigration to the UK*. CReAM discussion paper no. 22/13 University College London: Centre for Research and Analysis of Migration.

212 Brandariz Garcia, J. A. and Fernandez Bessa, C. (2011). The construction of migrants as a risk category in the Spanish penal system. In Palidda, S., ed., *Racial criminalization of migrants in the 21st century*. Farnham: Ashgate.

213 Polychroniou, C. J. (2017). Exposing the myths of neoliberal capitalism. *Truthout*. 8 February. http://www.truth-out.org/opinion/item/39393-exposing-the-myths-of-neoliberal-capitalism-an-interview-with-ha-joon-chang

214 Clarke, J. and Newman, J. (2012). The alchemy of austerity. *Critical Social Policy* 32 (3): 299–319.

215 Shilliam, R. (2018). *Race and the undeserving poor*, pp. 9–12. Newcastle: Agenda Publishing.

216 Gottfried, G. and Lawton, K. (2011). *In-work poverty in the recession.* Briefing note. London: IPPR; Wills, J. and Linneker, B. (2013). In-work poverty and the living wage in the United Kingdom: a geographical perspective. *Transactions of the Institute of British Geographers*, p. 38.

217 Welfare Reform Act. (2012).

218 Burns, G. (1978). TV interview for Granada *World in Action.* 27 January. https://www.margaretthatcher.org/document/103485

219 Malik, N. (2019). *We need new stories*, pp. 53–94. London: Weidenfeld & Nicolson.

220 Gilroy, P. (2004). *After empire: melancholia or convivial culture?* Abingdon: Routledge.

221 Ware, V. (2012). *Military migrants: fighting for YOUR country.* Basingstoke: Palgrave.

222 ONS. (2013). *Table KS201EW: 2011 Census: Ethnic group, local authorities in England and Wales*, ONS; Nandi, A. and L. Platt. (2012). How diverse is the UK? in *Understanding Society 2*, Swindon: ESRC; Nandi, A. and L. Platt. (2013). *Britishness and identity assimilation among the UK's minority and majority ethnic groups.* Understanding Society Working Paper Series No. 2013–08, December 2013.

223 Home Office. (2002). *Secure Borders, Safe Haven.* London: HMSO; Squire, V. (2005). Integration with diversity in modern Britain: New Labour on nationality, immigration and asylum. *Journal of Political Ideologies* 10(1): 51–74.

224 Castles, S. et. al. (2002). *Integration: mapping the field.* Home Office online report 29/03.

225 Council of the European Union. (2004). *Press release: Common basic principles on immigrant integration*, p. 17. 19 November.

226 Rogaly, B. and Taylor, B. (2010). They called them communists then... what d'you call 'em now?... insurgents? Narratives of British military expatriates in the context of the new imperialism. *Journal of Ethnic and Migration Studies.* 36(8): 1335–1351.

227 Garner, S. (2007). The European Union and the racialisation of immigration, 1986–2006. *Race/Ethnicity: Multidisciplinary Global Contexts*, 1(1): 61–87.

228 ONS. (2013). *Op. cit.*

229 Hill, C. (1963). *West Indian migrants and London churches.* London: OUP; Kalilombe, P. (1997). Black Christianity in Britain. *Ethnic and Racial Studies* 20(2): 306–324.

230 Jenkins, R. (1967). *Essays and speeches*, p. 267. London: Collins.
231 Squire, V. (2005). *Op. cit.*, p. 71.
232 Essed, P. (1991). *Understanding everyday racism*, pp. 39–44. London: Sage.
233 Castel, R. (2003). L'insecurite sociale. Qu'est-ce qu' etre protégé? Paris: Seuil/La republique des idees.
234 Bonnett, A. (1998). How the British working class became white: the symbolic (re)formation of racialised capitalism, *Journal of Historical Sociology*, 11(3): 316–340.
235 Virdee, S. (2014). *Racism, class and the racialised outsider*. Basingstoke: Palgrave MacMillan.
236 Garner, S. (2016). *A moral economy of whiteness: four frames of racialising discourse*. Abingdon: Routledge; Kelley, R. D. G. (2013). Resisting the war against the Black and Brown underclass. *Counterpunch*, 25 November.
237 Koram, K. and Nisancioglu, K. (2017). *Britain: The Empire that never was*. http://criticallegalthinking.com/2017/10/31/britain-empire-never/
238 Barlow, D. H. and Durand, V. M. (2005). *Abnormal psychology: integrative approaches*. London: Thompson Learning; Cashdan, S. (1972). *Abnormal psychology*. Englewood Cliffs, NJ: Prentice Hall; Andrews, K. (2016). The psychosis of whiteness: the celluloid hallucinations of Amazing Grace and Belle. *Journal of Black Studies*. DOI:10.1177/0021934716638802 https://journals.sagepub.com/doi/full/10.1177/0021934716638802
239 Bhambra, G. K. (2009). *Rethinking modernity*, p. 5. Basingstoke: Palgrave Macmillan.
240 Karenga, M. (1993). *Introduction to black studies*, second edition, p. 35. Los Angeles, CA: The University of Sankore Press.
241 Rattansi, A. (2011). *Multiculturalism: a very short introduction*, pp. 153–4. Oxford: OUP; Hall, S. (1992). The West and the Rest: discourse and power, pp. 275–331, in Hall S. and Gieben, B., eds., *Formations of modernity*. Cambridge: Polity Press.
242 Subrahmanyam, S. (1997). Connected histories: notes towards a reconfiguration of early modern Eurasia, p. 748. *Modern Asian Studies* 31/3; Abu-Lughod, J. (1989). *Beyond European hegemony: the world system AD 1250–1350*, pp. 353–73. Oxford: OUP.
243 Eisenstein, E. (1969). The advent of printing and the problem of the Renaissance, p. 46. *Past and Present* 45, November; Sabra, A. L. (1947). The Andalusian revolt against Ptolemaic astronomy:

Averroes and Al-Bitruji, in Mendelsohn, E., ed., *Transformation and tradition in the sciences: Essays in honour of I. Bernard Cohen*, p. 138. Cambridge: CUP; Joll, J. (1980). Europe – an historian's view, p. 8. *History of European Ideas* 1/1; Gilmore, M. P. (1952). *The world of humanism 1453–1517*, p. 187. New York, NY: Harper and Row.

244 Jardine, L. (1996). *Worldly goods: a new history of the Renaissance.* London: Papermac; Jardine, L. and Brotton, J. (2000). *Global interests: Renaissance art between East and West*, pp. 8, 61, 133. London: Reaktion Books.

245 Perlin, F. (1994). *Unbroken landscape: commodity, category, sign and identity*, p. 98. Hampshire: Variorum; Bernal, M. (1987). *Black Athena*, Volume 1, p. 156. London: Free Association Books; Harding, S. (1998). *Is science multicultural? Postcolonialisms, Feminisms and Epistemologies*, pp. 31, 36. Bloomington, IN: Indiana UP.

246 Rodriguez-Salgado, M. J. (1998). Christians, Civilized and Spanish: multiple identities in sixteenth century Spain, reprinted from *The Transactions of the Royal Historical Society 6th Series*, 8, pp. 233–51; Yapp, M. E. (1992). Europe in the Turkish Mirror *Past and Present: The cultural and political construction of Europe* 137, November, pp. 134–55; Lewis, A. R. (1990). The Islamic World and the Latin West, 1350–1500 *Speculum* 65/4, pp. 833–44.

247 Broers, M. (1989). Italy and the modern state: the experience of Napoleonic rule, pp. 137, 489, 492, in Furet, F. and Ozouf, M., eds., *The French Revolution and the creation of modern political culture. Vol. 3: The transformation of political culture 1789–1849.* Oxford: Pergamon; Dubois, L. (2004). *A colony of citizens: revolution and slave emancipation in the French Caribbean, 1787–1804.* Chapel Hill, NC: University of North Carolina Press.

248 Chatterjee, P. (1986). Nationalist thought and the colonial world, p. 30. London: Zed; Cohn, B. S. and Dirks, N. B. (1988). Beyond the fringe: the nation-state, colonialism and the technologies of power. *Journal of Historical Sociology* 1/2, 224–8; Bayly, C. A. (1993). Knowing the country: Empire and Information in India. *Modern Asian Studies Special Issue: How social, political and cultural information is collected, defined, used and analyzed* 27/1, pp. 2–43; Viswanathan, G. (1989). *Masks of conquest: Literary study and British rule in India*, pp. 3, 23. New York, NY: Columbia UP.

249 Crafts, N. F. R. (1985). *British economic growth during the Industrial Revolution*, pp. 69, 116, 142–6, 151–2. Oxford: Clarendon; Beckert, S. (2014). *Empire of cotton*, pp. 7, 32, 35, 45–55. London: Penguin.

250 Findlay, R. and O'Rourke, K. H. (2007). *Power and plenty*, pp. 319–20, 330–45. Princeton, NJ: Princeton UP; Findlay, R. (1982). Trade and growth in the Industrial Revolution, in Kindleberger, C. P. and di Tella, G., eds., *Economics in the long view: Essays in honour of W. W. Rostow, volume 1, Models and Methodology*. London: Macmillan; Solow, B. L. (2014). *The economic consequences of the Atlantic slave trade*. Lanham, MD: Lexington.

251 Oppenheim, A. L. (1964). *Ancient Mesopotamia*. Chicago, IL: Chicago UP; Thapar, R. (1966). *A history of India*. Harmondsworth: Penguin; Khaldun, I. (1967) [1377], *Al-Muqaddimah*. Beirut: UNESCO; Lancel, S. (1997). *Carthage: a history*, p. 118. Oxford: Blackwell; Goody, J. (2006). *The theft of history*, pp. 50–4. Cambridge: CUP.

252 Quoted in Yalman, N. O. (2001). Further observations on love (or equality), p. 271, in Warner, J., ed., *Cultural horizons*. Syracuse, NY: Syracuse UP; Rattansi, A. (2011). *Op. cit.*, p. 155.

253 Malinowski, B. (1947). *Crime and custom in savage society*. London: Kegan Paul; Evans-Pritchard, E. E. (1940). *The Nuer*. Oxford: Clarendon; Schapera, I. (1938). *A handbook of Tswana law and custom*. Oxford: OUP; Goody, J. (2006). *Op. cit.*, p. 59; Gluckman, M. (1955). *The judicial process among the Barotse of Northern Rhodesia*. Manchester: Manchester UP.

254 Rattansi, A. (2011). *Op. cit.*, p. 155; Goody, J. (2006). *Op. cit.*, pp. 241–3.

255 Yalman, N. O. (2001). *Op. cit.*, p. 277; Hopkins, T. J. (1966). The social teaching of the Bhagavata Purana, in Singer, M., ed., *Krishna: myths, rites and attitudes*. Honolulu, HI: East-West Center.

256 Kymlica, W. (2007). *Multicultural odysseys*. Oxford: OUP.

257 Bottero, J. (1987). *Mesopotamie: l'ecriture, la raison et les dieux*, pp. 113 ff., 157, 168. Paris; Factor, R. L. (1983). What is the logic in Buddhist logic? *Philosophy East and West* 33:2, 187; Goody, J. (1996). *The East in the West*, pp. 11–25. Cambridge, CUP.

258 Hesse, B. (2007). Racialized modernity: an analytics of white mythologies. *Ethnic and Racial Studies*, 30(4): 643–663; Young, R. J. C. (1990). *White mythologies*. London: Routledge.

259 Gopal, P. (2019). *Insurgent Empire: anticolonial resistance and British dissent*, pp. 6–18. London: Verso; Olusoga, D. (2016). *Black and British: a forgotten history*, pp. xx–xxi. London: Macmillan; Bhambra, G. K. (2009). *Op. cit.*

260 Department for Education. (2021). *Schools, pupils and their characteristics, 2019/20*. 2 February. https://explore-education-statistics.service.

gov.uk/find-statistics/school-pupils-and-their-characteristics; Choudry, S. (2021). *Op. cit.*, p. 111. St. Albans: Critical Publishing.

261 Department for Education. (2021). *GCSE results ('Attainment 8'), 2019/20.* 6 April. https://www.ethnicity-facts-figures.service.gov.uk/education-skills-and-training/11-to-16-years-old/gcse-results-attainment-8-for-children-aged-14-to-16-key-stage-4/latest

262 Bhopal, K. (2018). *White privilege: the myth of a post-racial society*, pp. 74–6. Bristol: Policy Press.

263 Department for Education. (2020). *Apprenticeship starts by ethnicity compared with the overall population, 2018/19.* 11 November. https://www.ethnicity-facts-figures.service.gov.uk/education-skills-and-training/a-levels-apprenticeships-further-education/apprenticeship-starts/latest

264 HESA. (2020). *UK domiciled HE pupil enrolments by ethnicity, 2019/20.* https://www.hesa.ac.uk/data-and-analysis/pupils/table-5

265 HESA Student Record. (2021). *UK undergraduate degree results, 2019/20.* 2 August. https://www.ethnicity-facts-figures.service.gov.uk/education-skills-and-training/higher-education/undergraduate-degree-results/latest

266 HESA staff record, 2017–18. Cited in Universities UK (2019). *Op. cit.*, p. 15.

267 *Ibid.*, pp. 123–4; Bhopal, K. (2018). *Op. cit.*, pp. 52–5.

268 Byrne, B. et al., eds. (2020). *Op. cit.*, p. 94.

269 Shain, F. (2013). Race, nation and education, *Education Inquiry*, 4:1, 63–85, DOI: 10.3402/edui.v4i1.22062

270 e.g. Swann, Lord. (1985). *Education for all.* Command paper 9453. London: Her Majesty's Stationery Office; Rampton Report. (1981). *West Indian children in our schools.* London: Her Majesty's Stationery Office.

271 e.g. Rhamie, J. (2013). Black academic success: what's changed? In Bhopal, K. and Maylor, U., eds., *Educational inequalities in schools and higher education*, pp. 47–64. New York and London: Routledge; Nehaul, K. (1996). *The schooling of children of Caribbean heritage.* Stoke-on-Trent: Trentham; Coard, B. (1971). *How the West Indian child is made educationally subnormal in the British school system.* London: New Beacon.

272 e.g. Gillborn, D. (2008). *Racism and education: coincidence or conspiracy?* London: Routledge; Crozier, G. (2005). There's war against our children. *British Journal of Sociology of Education*, 26 (5), 585–598.

273 Byfield, C. (2008). *Black boys can make it.* Stoke: Trentham.

274 Maylor, U. (2014). *Teacher training and the education of black children*, pp. 13–36. Abingdon: Routledge; Strand, S. (2012). The White British-Black Caribbean achievement gap: Tests, tiers and teacher expectations. *British Educational Research Journal* 38 (1): 75–101; Yosso, T. J. (2005). Whose culture has capital? *Race, Ethnicity and Education* 8 (1): 69–91; Bourdieu, P. and Passeron, J-C. (1979). *The Inheritors*. Chicago, IL: University of Chicago Press.

275 Gillborn, D. (2016). Education policy as an act of white supremacy, p. 46. In Taylor, E. et al., eds., *Foundations of Critical Race Theory in Education*, 2nd edition. New York, NY: Routledge.

276 Knowles, E. and Ridley, W. (2006). *Another spanner in the works*, pp. 1–2, 13. Stoke: Trentham.

277 King, J. E. (1995). Culture-centered knowledge, in Banks, J and Banks, C. M., eds., *Handbook of research on multicultural education*, pp. 276–7. New York, NY: Macmillan; Wynter, S. (1992). *Do not call us Negros: how 'multicultural' textbooks perpetuate racism*, p. 17. San Francisco, CA: Aspire.

278 Maylor, U. et al. (2009). *Black children's achievement programme evaluation*. Research Report 177. Nottingham: Department for Children, Schools and Families.

279 Coard, B. (1971, rprtd. 2005). How the West Indian child is made educationally subnormal in the British school system. In Richardson, B., ed., *Tell it like it is: how our schools fail Black children*, pp. 27–59. London: Bookmarks.

280 Clark, K. B. and Clark, M. P. (1940). Skin colour as a factor in racial identification and preferences in Negro children. *Journal of Experimental Education* 8 161–163.

281 Andrews, K. (2013). *Op. cit.*, pp. 4–7.

282 Swann, Lord. (1985). *Op. cit.*

283 Rampton, A. (1981). *West Indian children in our schools*. Cmnd 8273. London: HMSO.

284 Joseph, Sir K. (1985). The Secretary of State for Education and Science. HC Deb 14 March vol 75 cc 451–9

285 Begum, H. *Trying to divide white and ethnic minority working class people helps no one*. https://www.theguardian.com/commentisfree/2021/jan/25/divide-white-ethnic-minority-working-class-government; Gillborn, D. (2008). *Racism and education: coincidence or conspiracy?* pp. 53–8. Abingdon: Routledge.

286 Department for Education. (2012). *Teachers' Standards*. London: Department for Education.

287 Castro, A. (2010). Themes in the research on pre-service teachers' views on cultural diversity. *Educational Researcher* 39 (3) 198–210; Lander, A. K. (2014). Initial teacher education: the practice of whiteness, p. 99. In Race, R. and Lander, A. K., eds., *Advancing race and ethnicity in education*. Basingstoke: Palgrave Macmillan.

288 UK NGO's alternative report, drafted by The Runnymede Trust. (2016). *Submission to the UN Committee on the Elimination of Racial Discrimination* (ICERD, ed.) *with regard to the UK Government's 21st to 23rd Periodic Reports*, pp. 1, 8, 16–18, 83. https://runnymedetrust.org/uploads/CERD%20Civil%20Society%20Report%20UKfinal.pdf

289 Eddo-Lodge, R. (2017). *Op. cit.*, pp. 81-4.

290 Lord Swann. (1985). *Education for all*, Cmnd. 9453, pp. 26-7. London: Her Majesty's Stationery Office.

291 Demie, F. (2019). *Educational inequality*, pp. xv, 204. London: IOE Press.

292 Boakye, J. (2018). *Hold tight*, pp. 223, 344, 356. London: Influx.

293 Lander, A. K. (2014). *Op. cit.*, p. 96.

294 Department for Education. 2012. *Initial Teacher Training (ITT) Criteria*, p. 4. London: Department for Education; Department for Education. (2013). *Schools Direct*. London: Department for Education; Furlong, J. et al. (2000). *Teacher education in transition*. Buckingham: Open University.

295 Gaine, C. (1995). *Still no problem here*. Stoke: Trentham; Menter, I. (1989). Teaching practice stasis: racism, sexism and school experience in initial teacher education, *British Journal of Sociology of Education*, 10 (4), 459–473.

296 Burbank, M. et al. (2010). *I feel your pain*. Paper presented at the American Educational Research Association conference, 30 April–2 May, Denver, Colorado; Flowers, T. and Flowers, L. (2008). Factors affecting urban African-American high school pupils' achievement in reading, 43 (2), *Urban Education*, 154–171.

297 TDA (Training and Development Agency for Schools). (2005). *Annual survey of newly qualified teachers*. London: TDA; TTA (Teacher Training Agency). (2007). *Annual survey of newly qualified teachers*. London: TTA.

298 Maylor, U. ((2014). *Teacher training and the education of black children*, pp. 65–84. Abingdon: Routledge; Lander, A. K. (2014). *Op. cit.*, pp. 94–9.

299 Roithmayr, D. (2003). Locked in inequality: the persistence of discrimination, *Michigan Journal of Race and Law*, 9: 38; Roithmayr, D.

(2004). Locked in segregation, *Virginia Journal of Social Policy and the Law*, 12(2): 197.

300 Gillborn, D. (2008). *Racism and education: Coincidence or conspiracy?* pp. 67–8, 88-9. Abingdon: Routledge.

301 Brighouse, Sir T. (2021). Foreword, pp. xiii-xiv, in Choudry, S. *Op. cit.;* Gillborn, D. (2008). *Op. cit.*, pp. 110–7.

302 ONS. (2015). 2011 census analysis: ethnicity and religion of the non-UK born population in England and Wales. 18 June. https://www.ons.gov.uk/peoplepopulationandcommunity/culturalidentity/ethnicity/articles/2011censusanalysisethnicityandreligionofthenonukbornpopulationinenglandandwales/2015-06-18

303 Gaine, C. (2005). *We're all white thanks*, pp. 6–7. Stoke: Trentham.

304 Gaine, C. (1995). *Op. cit.*, pp. 2, 3.

305 Gaine, C. (1995). *Op. cit.*, pp., 7, 14.

306 *Ibid.*, pp. 124–49.

307 Department for Education (2014). *The Equality Act and schools*, p. 5. London: DfE.

308 Bhopal, K. (2018). *Op. cit.*, pp. 4, 70–3.

309 Bhopal, K. (2018). *Op. cit.*, pp. 66–76, 80–5; Lander, A. K. (2014). *Op. cit.*, pp. 98–9.

310 Ladson-Billings, G. (2006). AERA Presidential Address. From the achievement gap to the education debt: understanding achievement in US schools. *Educational Researcher*, Oct., Vol. 35, No. 7, pp. 3–12.

311 Baldwin, J. (1961). *The negro in American culture*, a group discussion. the post-archive https://www.youtube.com/watch?v=jNpitdJSXWY

312 Department for Education. (2020). School teacher workforce, 2018. 7 September. www.ethnicity-facts-figures.service.gov.uk/workforce-and-business/workforce-diversity/school-teacher-workforce/latest

313 Joseph-Salisbury, R. (2020). *Race and racism in English secondary schools*, pp. 5, 7–9. London: Runnymede Trust.

314 Eddo-Lodge, R. (2018). *Op. cit.*, pp. 90–8.

315 DfE. (2020). *School workforce in England 2018, by ethnicity.* 7 September. https://www.ethnicity-facts-figures.service.gov.uk/workforce-and-business/workforce-diversity/school-teacher-workforce/latest :Lander, A. K. (2014). Initial teacher education: the practice of whiteness, p. 107. In Race, R. and Lander, A. K., eds., *Advancing race and ethnicity in education.* Basingstoke: Palgrave Macmillan.

316 Lander, A. K. (2010). Race encounters in ITE: tutors' narratives on race equality and initial teacher education, unpublished EdD thesis, p. 49. Institute of Education, London University.
317 Marx, S. (2006). *Revealing the invisible: confronting passive racism in teacher education*, p. 6. New York, NY: Routledge.
318 Lander, A. K. (2010). *Op. cit.*, pp. 85–100.
319 Picower, B. (2009). The unexamined Whiteness of teaching: how White teachers maintain and enact dominant racial ideologies. *Race, Ethnicity and Education*, 12:2, 197–215.
320 Department for Education. (2020). School Direct. https://getintoteaching.education.gov.uk/explore-my-options/teacher-training-routes/school-led-training/school-direct-salaried
321 Anderson, K. J. (2010). *Benign bigotry: the psychology of subtle prejudice*, p. 250. Cambridge: CUP.
322 Marx, S. (2006). *Op. cit.*, pp. 67–71.
323 Wilkins, C. and Lall, R. (2010). Getting by or getting on? Black pupil teachers' experiences of teacher education, *Race Equality Teaching*, 28 (2), 19–26.
324 Lander, A. K. (2015). Racism - it's part of my everyday life: black and minority ethnic pupils' experiences in a predominantly white school. In Alexander, C. et al., eds., *Race, education and inequality in contemporary Britain*, pp. 32–5. London: Runnymede Trust.
325 Gay, G. (2018). *Culturally responsive teaching*. Third Edition, pp. 29–36. New York, NY: Teachers' College, Columbia University; Ladson-Billings, G. (1994). Who will teach our children? pp. 132–3. In Hollins, E. R., King, J. E. and Hayman, W. C., eds., *Teaching diverse populations: formulating a knowledge base*. Albany, NY: State University of New York Press.
326 Ryan, W. (1971). Blaming the victim. New York, NY: Random House. Cited in Gay, G. (1983). Multiethnic education: historical developments and future prospects. *Phi Delta Kappan*, 64(8), 560–563.
327 Baptiste, H. P. (1979). Multicultural education: a synopsis, p. 11. Lanham, MD: University Press of America. Cited in King, J. E. et al., eds., (1997). *Preparing teachers for cultural diversity*, pp. 9–10. New York, NY: Teachers College, Columbia University.
328 Goodwin, A. L. (1997). Historical and contemporary perspectives on multicultural teacher education, pp. 17–21. In King J. E. et al., eds., *Ibid.*

329 Helms, J. E. (1990). *Black and white racial identity*. Westport, CT: Greenwood.

330 ONS. (2013). *Immigration patterns of non-UK born populations in England and Wales in 2011*. Newport: ONS.

331 Olusoga, D. (2017). *Op. cit.*, pp. xx–xxi.

332 McPhail, I. P. (1994). Foreword, p. viii. In Hollins, E. R., King, J. E. and Hayman, W. C., eds., *Op. cit.;* Thiong'o, N. G. (1981, rprtd. 2005). *Decolonising the mind*, pp. 2–25. Woodbridge/Portsmouth, NH: James Currey/ Heinemann.

333 e.g. Bunce, R. and Field, P. (2017). *Renegade: the life and times of Darcus Howe*. London: Bloomsbury.

334 Bell, D. (1987). *And we are not saved: the elusive quest for racial justice*, p. 250. New York, NY: Basic Books; Wilcox, P. (1970). Educating for black humanism, p. 11. In Wright, N., ed., *What black educators are saying*. San Francisco, CA: Leswing Press.

335 Choudry, S. (2021). *Op. cit.*, pp. 99–112.

336 Stokes L. et al. (2015). A c*ompendium of evidence on ethnic minority resilience to the effects of deprivation on attainment*. London: DfE.

337 www.ourmigrationstory.org.uk ; Kara, B. (2020). *A little guide for teachers: diversity in schools*. London: SAGE; www.history.org.uk/ha-news/news/297/new-resources-for-teaching-black-british-history-a; https://files.royalhistsoc.org/wp-content/uploads/2018/10/17205337/RHS_race_report_EMBARGO_0001180ct.pdf ; www.theblackcurriculum.com/

338 Available on Teach Indus at http://old.harappa.com/teach/index.html and www.harappa.com/resources.

339 www.bbc.co.uk/programmes/p05b5fdg; www.bbc.co.uk/newsround/46428985; http://news.bbc.co.uk/1/hi/world/south_asia/1751044.stm; www.banglastories,org; https://partitionededucationgroup.wordpress.com/; www.southasianheritage.org.uk

340 www.1001inventions.com/fun-learning/educational-materials/

341 www.natre.org.uk/about-natre/projects/anti-bullying; www.runnymedetrust.org/currentPublications/publications-by-category/education-and-young-people.html; www.theredcard.org/resources-and-activities; https://equaliteach.co.uk/for-schools/classroom-resources; www.equalityhumanrights.com/en/secondary-education-resources; email HateCrimeSchoolsProject@cps.gov.uk; www.kickitout.org/Pages/FAQs/Category/education-toolkits

342 Page et al. (2007). *Engaging effectively with black and minority ethnic parents in children's and parental services.* London: DCSF.
343 www.ippr.org/publications/saturdays-for-success; www.supplementary education.org.uk/
344 https://thelinkingnetwork.org.uk/
345 Chetty, D. and Sands-O'Connor, K. (2018). http://booksforkeeps.co.uk/issue228/childrens-books/articles/beyond-the-secret-garden-part-one-the-fantasy-of-story
346 Ladson-Billings, G. (1992). Reading between the lines and beyond the pages: a culturally relevant approach to literacy teaching. *Theory into Practice, 31,* 312–320.
347 Arshad, R. et al. (2020). *Social justice re-examined.* Revised edition, pp. 118–20. London: UCL IOE Press; Ladson-Billings, G. (1995). But that's just good teaching! The case for culturally relevant pedagogy. *Theory into Practice*, 34 (3), 160.
348 Crawford, E. E. and Troeger, T. H. (1995). *The hum: call and response in African-American preaching.* Nashville, TN: Abingdon.
349 De Lacey, A. (2015). *Deeper than rap: Grime is not a subgenre of Hip-Hop*, pp. 6, 8, 9. https://www.complex.com/pigeons-and-planes/2015/11/grime-hip=hop; Andr*ews, K. (2013). Op. cit.*, p. 36.
350 Culture circles: Freire, P. (1970, rprtd. 2017). *Pedagogy of the oppressed*, pp. 37, 52 ff. London: Penguin. Cogen dialogues: Tobin, K. G. and Roth, W.-M. (2006). *Teaching to learn: a view from the field.* Rotterdam: Sense.
351 Kathryn Au's work with Hawaiians and Carol Lee's work with African-American youth. In Cole, M. (2010). What's culture got to do with it? *Educational Researcher* 39, no. 6: 461–70.
352 DfE. (2020). *School workforce in England, 2018, by ethnicity.* 7 September.
353 #RickRoss #Hustlin #Vevo (2009). Rick Ross - *Hustlin'* (Official Video). https://www.youtube.com/watch?v=JU9TouRnO84
354 Bourdieu, P. (1983). 'Forms of capital' in J. C. Richards, ed., *Handbook of Theory and Research for the Sociology of Education*, p. 249. New York, NY: Greenwood Press.
355 Portes, A. and Landolt, P. (1996). The downside of social capital. *American Prospect*, 94, no. 26: 18–21.
356 Boakye, J. (2018). *Op. cit.*, p. 28.; Rosso, F. (1981, uploaded 2019). *Babylon.* Jah guide and protect. https://www,youtube.com/watch?v=PUKzUNhhzDo.
357 Bourdieu, P. and Wacquant, L. (1992). *An invitation to reflexive sociology.* Chicago, IL: University of Chicago Press.

358 Walker, E. N. (2014). *Beyond Banneker: black mathematicians and the paths to excellence*, p. xi. Albany, NY: SUNY Press; Gates, H. L. Jr. (1988, rprtd. 2014). *The signifying monkey*, pp.49–56. New York, NY: OUP.

359 Emdin, C. (2016). *For white folks who teach in the hood … and the rest of y'all too: Reality Pedagogy and urban education.* Boston, MA: Beacon Press.

360 Home Affairs Committee. (2019). *Serious youth violence: Sixteenth report of sessions 2017–19.* London: House of Commons. https://publications.parliament.uk/pa/cm201719/cmselect/cmhaff/1016/1016.pdf; Office of the Children's Commissioner. (2019). *Guess how much we love you: why politicians urgently need to help our children.* London: Office for the Children's Commissioner. www.childrenscommissioner.gov.uk/wp-content/uploads/2019/09/cco-a-manifesto-for-children.pdf

361 Bradford, B. and Tiratelli, M. (2019). *Does stop and search reduce crime?* UK Justice policy review focus 4. London: Centre for Crime and Justice Studies; Long, L. (2018). *Perpetual suspects: a critical race theory of black and mixed-race experiences of policing.* London: Palgrave.

362 Graham, K. (2016). The British school-to-prison pipeline. In Andrews, K. and Palmer, L., eds., *Blackness in Britain*, pp. 130–42. Abingdon: Routledge; Gillborn, D. (2008). *Op. cit.*, pp. 60–3.

363 Alexander, C. and Shankley, W. (2020). In Byrne, B. et al. *Op. cit.*, p. 93; ACPO. (2013). *Prevent, Police and Schools. Helping schools stay safe: guidance for police officers and police staff.* London: ACPO.

364 Henshall, A. (2018). Are police officers in schools a force for good? *Schools Week.* 26 May. https://schoolsweek.co.uk/are-police-officers-in-schools-a-force-for-good; Joseph-Salisbury, R. (2020). *Op. cit.*, pp. 14–16.

365 McIntyre, N., N. Parveen and Thomas, T. (2021). UK police forces deploy 683 officers in schools with some poorer areas targeted. *The Guardian.* 25 March.

366 Department for Education. (2019). *Permanent exclusions by ethnicity, 2017/18.* https://www.gov.uk/government/statistics/permanent-and-fixed-period-exclusions-in-England-2017-to-2018;

Warde, B. (2013). Black male disproportionality in the criminal justice systems in the USA, Canada and England. *Journal of African-American Studies* 17 (4): 461–479.

367 Bourdieu, P. and Passeron, J. C. (1990). *Reproduction in education, society and culture.* 2nd edition. London: Sage; Bowles, S. and Gintis, H.

(2002). Schooling in capitalist America revisited, p. 1. *Sociology of Education* 75 (1): 1–18.

368 Macleod, J. (1995). *Ain't no makin' it: aspirations and attainment in a low income neighborhood,* p. 13. Boulder, CO: Westview Press.

369 Willis, P. (1977, rprtd. 2000). *Learning to labour: how working class kids get working class jobs*, p. 154. Aldershot: Ashgate.

370 Wacquant, L. (2010). Crafting the neoliberal state: workforce, prison fare and social insecurity. *Sociological Forum* 25 (2): 197–220.

371 Swain, A.E. and Noblit, G. W. (2011). Education in a punitive society: an introduction. *Urban Review* 43: 465–475; Davis, A. Y. (2003). *Are prisons obsolete?* p. 16. New York, NY: Seven Stories; Foucault, M. (1977, rprtd. 1991). *Discipline and punish.* London: Penguin Books.

372 Taylor, M. (2011). School's ban on boy's cornrows is 'indirect discrimination'. *The Guardian.* 17 June.

373 DfES. (2006). *Priority Review: Exclusion of black pupils. "Getting it. Getting it right"*, pp. 12–34.

374 Eastman, A. (2011). *No excuses: a review of educational exclusion.* Centre for Social Justice.

375 Scott, J. and Spencer, L. (2013). *School meets street: exploring the links between low achievement, school exclusion and youth crime among African-Caribbean boys in London.* (No. 2013–25). ISER Working Paper Series.

376 Graham, K. (2015). *Does school prepare men for prison? The life histories of eleven former prisoners.* Doctoral thesis. University of Birmingham.

377 Home Office (2013. *Preventing youth violence and gang involvement. Practical advice for schools and colleges* https://assets.publishing.service.gov.uk/government/uploads/system/uploads/attachment_data/file/418131/Preventing_youth_violence_and_gang_involvement_v3_March2015.pdf;_Gove. M. (2011). Speech to the Durand Academy. 1 September. https://www.michaelgove.com/news/michael-goves-speech-durand-academy

378 Clark, L. (2009). A quarter of all UK schools have their own police officer to crack-down on youth crime. *MailOnline* https://www.dailymail.co.uk/news/article-1104514/A-quarter-UK-schools-police-officer-crackdown-youth-crime.html

379 Police Foundation. (2011). Safer school partnerships. *The Briefing,* 2(2), November 2011. London: The Police Federation.

380 *Ibid.*, p.8; Case, S. (2006). Young people 'at risk' of what? Challenging risk-focused early intervention as crime prevention. *Youth Justice* 6(3), 171–179; Bowling, B. and Phillips, C. (2006). *Young black people and the*

criminal justice system. Submission to the House of Commons Home Office Committee Inquiry, October 2006.

381 Police Foundation. (2013). *Op. cit.*, p. 8; Pitts, J. (2014). Who dunnit? Gangs, Joint Enterprise, bad character and duress. *Youth & Policy* 113: 48–59.

382 Ministry of Justice. (2020). *Proven reoffending, by ethnicity, 2016/17*. 9th March. https://www.ethnicity-facts-figures.service.gov.uk/crime-justice-and-the-law/crime-and-reoffending/proven-reoffending/latest; Graham, K. (2015). *Op. cit.*, p. 161.

383 Alexander, C. et al. (2014). *The Runnymede School Report: Race, education and inequality in contemporary Britain*, p. 4. London: Runnymede Trust.

384 Tomlinson, S. (2014). 'Fundamental British values', p. 10. In *Ibid.*

385 Higgins. C. (2011). Historians say Michael Gove risks turning history lessons into propaganda classes. *The Guardian*. 17 August.

386 Leach, A. et al. (2020). Black British history: the row over the school curriculum in England. *The Guardian*. 13 July; Impact of Omission. (2020). *Survey*. https://impactofomission.squarespace.com/survey

387 Hart, A. R. (1985, rprtd. 2002). *Slaves who abolished slavery*. Kingston: University of the West Indies press.

388 Walker, R. (2006). *When we ruled*, pp. 557–69. London: Every Generation Media.

389 Jones, S. P. (2020) Ending curriculum violence. https://www.learningforjustice.org/magazine/spring-2020/ending-curriculum-violence; Bery, S. (2014). Multiculturalism, teaching slavery and white supremacy. *Equity and Excellence in Education*, Vol. 47. Issue 3. pp. 334–352.

390 Arday, J. (2021). *Black British history in the National Curriculu*m, p. 21. London: The Black Curriculum.

391 Joseph-Salisbury, R. (2020). *Op. cit.*, pp. 10, 12–3.

392 DfE. (2013). *History programmes of study: Key stage 3. National curriculum in England*, p. 1. https://assets.publishing.service.gov.uk/government/uploads/system/uploads/attachment_data/file/239075/SECONDARY_national_curriculum_-_History.pdf; DfE. (2014). *Promoting Fundamental British values as part of SMSC in schools: departmental advice for maintained schools*, p. 5. London: DfE.

393 McIntosh, K. et al. (2019). *Teaching migration, belonging and empire in secondary schools*. London: Tide/Runnymede Trust.

GLOSSARY

Advantage. A condition that puts someone in a superior position than others to achieve something.

Anti-intellectualism. Giving a person's own opinion on any issue without first considering what experts have written about that issue.

Anti-racist. Challenging racism so as to change the system and bring justice and equality in this generation.

Assimilate. For the person of colour to drop their own culture and adopt the culture of the white middle class.

Categorise. Distinguish people based on certain characteristics for the purpose of making generalisations about how to think about and engage with them.

Chip on your shoulder. Having a grievance that is likely to provoke a dispute, or feeling entitled or thinking too much of yourself.

Coalition to stop racism. People of colour encourage white people to focus on grievances their group has and work alongside people of colour on matters in which they have common ground.

Cogenerative/cogen dialogue. A dialogue between the teacher and four pupils representing classroom diversity and varieties of achievement. This decides how to deliver work content so as to meet pupil requirements.

Co-teaching. Under Reality Pedagogy, the two teachers are pupils. The teacher selects two pupils from the cogenerative dialogue and teaches them how to write a lesson plan and deliver its content. The pupils are graded based on their lesson methods. The teacher learns how to deliver work content from these pupils.

Coloniality or colonial matrix of power. A global system, imposed by the US and NATO to the present day, which has three aspects. Social power is determined by a person's skin colour, where light-skinned is most desirable and dark-skinned is least desirable. Countries wishing to advance, must do so by copying how

European countries became nation states – a Eurocentric requirement. Europeans are the best source of knowledge in everything.

Colour blind. A trick invented by Republicans to stop African Americans getting their civil rights at state level. To say that you don't see colour is, in reality, a white person's pretence that they're not racist. To people of colour, a white person saying they're colour-blind means they're trying to cover up their racial biases.

Competition/Grime battle. Pupils compete to find who the audience think is the best individual, using their culture to show their grasp of the work content. The emphasis is on participants writing a poem or chatting, so that the pupil is graded according to how they speak, rather than the traditional emphasis on studying and writing.

Context. A teacher needs to engage with the pupils' community and cultural context in order to increase pupils' confidence that the teacher understands their concerns.

Cosmopolitanism/cosmo duo. Using a teaching style that prioritises pupils' cultures. The teacher agrees roles that pupils will perform in the classroom, encouraging pupils' commitment to supporting their peers. The teacher uses language that pupils use in their community. To establish cosmo duos, the teacher starts by pairing academically stronger pupils with academically weaker pupils in the cogen group so that the stronger can help the weaker when work is more difficult.

Critical reflection. Ways of thinking that people of a different gender, class, age, sexuality or ethnic background have, which people can use to critique their own cultural ways of thinking and acting.

Curator. A manager who presents a museum's collections and interprets them to the public. A pupil can curate their life and classroom experiences via social media (whether real or on paper) to demonstrate to the teacher how well they are grasping the work content and their comments on it.

Discrimination puts prejudice into action. This happens when people go on to say or do something that shows to others that they discriminate against people of colour because they think themselves superior to people of colour.

Eurocentrism is a belief that certain events had world-changing consequences and that these events developed from within the culture and boundaries of Europe. This alleged uniqueness to the West means that these characteristics are believed to have universal relevance. Any non-Western nation is, therefore, only ever seen as belatedly catching up with the West and frowned upon if seen in some way to be deviant in its application of European models.

Hierarchy. An arrangement of objects or people positioned above or below each other.

Homicide. A human killing a human.

Identity. Being what a person is, including similarities between them and other people.

Ideology. A system of ideals and beliefs.

Implicit or unconscious bias. This is seen when people react in the heat of the moment based on their unconscious thinking, which has been produced by social conditioning and with which their conscious, rational thinking often struggles.

Integrate. For people of colour to change their culture a bit while white people change their culture a bit in order to meet somewhere in the middle. In practice, as a result of white people being unwilling to change their culture and practice, it effectively means people of colour are expected to assimilate into the white middle class.

Interculturalism. Discussing from, for example, an indigenous person's view of the world with someone speaking from a European view of the world. Show respect by expecting that a person should know more about their own continent than someone from a different continent.

Intersectionality refers to the multiple dimensions of black women's experiences, the experience of which is greater than the sum of race and gender.[lxxvi] People's lives can be affected by a number of additional axes of social division, e.g., class, sexuality, ability, citizenship status, Islamophobia, etc.

Lived experience. Lived experience is the experience of people on whom one or many social issues have had a personal impact.

Meritocracy. The argument that all people progress on merit, that success depends on how hard you're willing to work. However, this ignores the fact that meritocracy works in white people's favour and against people of colour and that it helps create inequalities in society.

Microaggressions. Microaggressions are everyday exchanges that send insulting messages to people because of the group they are seen to be a member of. While the speaker's intention might be for the very best of reasons and to compliment someone, the other person is left with not just a bad feeling but also a range of physical and mental health problems.

Neo-colonialism. Neo-colonialism is the use today of capitalism, cultural imperialism and conditional aid to direct the political and economic policies of other countries.

Oppression. Oppression takes place when one or a group imposes their will onto another or group in an unjust exercise of power.

Pedagogy. A method of teaching.

People of colour. People of African, Asian, Latin American or Pacific Islander backgrounds.

Playing the race card. Many people see racism as a type of card that people can play, rather like a joker. It's a card that's versatile and that can be used in any situation. Only people of colour play this card to say sorry for their personal failings. White people are unable to play the race card, in the same way that they can't be terrorists. The action of European empires in colonising most of the planet has not had any effect on shaping human history; it's just been people of colour playing cards.

Political correctness/PC. A term people apply to those who want more sensitivity shown towards a cause than others are willing to allow. It is a way to dismiss causes as frivolous, to justify ignoring them and their proponents. These causes are issues of justice for groups that are oppressed, e.g., women, people of colour, the poor, people with disabilities and GLBTQIA; they determine whether these groups feel they belong in society or not.

Postcolonial studies. Studies of the human consequences of European powers taking over the lands, labour and resources of lands that became part of their empire, written from their existing histories by people who had been colonised. As such, this is a critique of the history, culture, methods, literature and exploitation of those European powers and their people.

Post-racial society/post-race. A view that since people rarely see a noisy or violent case of racism, or since some people have had a black president, race must no longer be a significant factor in life.

Prejudice. Occurs when people think that they are superior to people of colour.

Race. There are no biological races. Unrelated people's DNA is 99.9 per cent the same. However, race is socially constructed as '[A] distinct biological type of human being, usually based on their skin colour or other physical characteristics.'

Racialisation is the process of assigning a racial identity to a group that didn't identify itself in this way.

Racial literacy. The ability to teach children and adults how to identify routine forms of racism and to develop strategies for countering it and coping with it.

Racism. Any programme or practice of discrimination, segregation, persecution or mistreatment based on a membership of a race or ethnic group. Cultural racism occurs when people stereotype people of colour's cultures, values and customs or their nature as permanently inferior. Individual racism involves discrimination in a person's relationships with people, whether known or unknown, that they meet informally on the street or in shops.

Ruling class. People who directly influence government and politics with the use of power or wealth, including billionaires.

Social construct A social construct is a value assigned to something based on the collective decision within a society rather than on a natural or independent existence. For example, money is pieces of paper and metal that have no value in themselves. Society agrees that these particular pieces of paper and metal are money and everyone as a result treats them as money.

Standpoint. People arrive at different standpoints through their different lived experiences. Lived experience is the experience of people on whom one or many social issues have had a personal impact.

Stereotype. Oversimplified view of a particular type of person.

Structural racism. Structural racism is a form of racism expressed in the practice of social and political institutions. It is reflected in disparities in, for example, wealth, income, criminal justice, employment, housing, health care, political power and education. People should prioritise ending structural racism over ending individual racism.

'the Other'. 'the Other' is what or who is not part of the individual Self. When 'the Other' does not fit with the norms of the majority social group, that person is disenfranchised and pushed to the margins of society.

Trauma is damage to a person's mind resulting from one event or more causing amounts of stress that are greater than the person can cope with. In time, this leads to serious, long-term consequences

Underachievement. A person who does not do as well as their peers from other ethnic groups.

Universalism. A belief that some ideas have universal application, especially the ideas of white men.

Whiteness. Whiteness is the effect of racism on the people who are racist. Whiteness has three linked dimensions: a place of structurally embedded advantage over people of colour, a standpoint from which white people look at themselves, others and the world and a range of cultural practices that white people both do not notice and make obscure. For many, their whiteness is most clearly seen through their feelings about Brexit.

White racial frame. The white racial frame is a white worldview including racial stereotypes, interpretations and narratives, reactions to accents and inclinations to discriminate.

White structurally embedded advantage means that if you're white your life will be positively impacted by being part of the white racial group at least once and possibly every day. Probably without you ever being aware of it.

White supremacy. The economic, political and cultural system that has made today's world. A system in which white people control power and material resources. In which ideas and thoughts about white superiority and entitlement are everywhere. And in which relationships between dominant white people and subordinate people of colour are acted out daily across institutions and social settings.

ACKNOWLEDGEMENTS

I acknowledge my dependence on those people who first led me to understand the different standpoints of people of colour through mentoring me: Dean Pusey, Les Isaac, Len Davis and the late David Greaves and Philip Mohabir.

I thank Michael Williams, Cindy Soso and Sam M. Amalemba for their work at BIS Publishing Services in publishing my first book, *Changing Generations*. I thank Michael for convening a meeting at City Hall, London, where the view of the meeting members was that I should produce a version of *Changing Generations*, 'but for schools'.

I thank Kim Cross, Dean Zaltsman, Kathryn Hodge, Julie Scott, Becky Banning and Cath Harris of Grosvenor House Publishing for all their help and professionalism in delivering a first-class book for everyone.

I value those in community groups across Wandsworth borough who have moulded my thinking, including Wale and Modupe Afolabi, Caesar Antonypillai, Delroy Powell, Freddie Brown, David and Sally Dean, Edward Maliki, Osoba Otaigbe, Noel and Sharon McLean, Steven and Gerard Patchaye, Imam Suliman Gani, Razia Shariff, Malik Gul, Kofi Mawuli Klu, Jayesh Patel, Len Rowe, Jonathan Swaby and Kwasi Gambrah.

I would like to thank staff at Kingston University and the University of London's School of Oriental and African Studies for permission to use their library reference materials.

I thank Dr R. David Muir, senior lecturer, School of Humanities, Roehampton University and 2001–3 deputy chairman of the Metropolitan Police Authority, for reading this book and for his comments on it.

I thank Dr Maria James, programme director for the PGCHE, senior lecturer and teaching fellow, School of Education, Theology and Leadership, St Mary's University, Twickenham for her comments on the teaching chapters.

I thank Dr Marika Sherwood and Michael Ohajuru for their comments on my writing style.

Thanks also go to Jenny Dyke and Sue Jelfs and their students for their enthusiasm at discussing some of the contents and for all their comments.

I thank Rach and Zac for their comments on the teaching chapters during their busy teaching schedules.

Thanks again to Norma for her patience with my non-availability while wrestling with what to write.

Thanks also to my mentor, Tom Chacko, for his inspiration and wisdom. The gems are most likely his. Any errors are mine alone!

Index

CPSIA information can be obtained
at www.ICGtesting.com
Printed in the USA
LVHW011543120122
708226LV00008BA/940